# The Dynamics
# of Emerging Ethnicities

Johan Leman (ed.)

# The Dynamics of Emerging Ethnicities

Immigrant and indigenous ethnogenesis
in confrontation

2nd revised edition

PETER LANG

Frankfurt am Main · Berlin · Bern · Bruxelles · New York · Oxford · Wien

Die Deutsche Bibliothek - CIP-Einheitsaufnahme

The dynamics of emerging ethnicities : immigrant and
indigenous ethnogenesis in confrontation / Johan Leman (ed.).
2nd revised edition. - Frankfurt am Main ; Berlin ; Bern ;
Bruxelles ; New York ; Oxford ; Wien : Lang, 2000
  ISBN 3-631-36477-6

ISBN 3-631-36477-6
US-ISBN 0-8204-4769-2

© Peter Lang GmbH
Europäischer Verlag der Wissenschaften
Frankfurt am Main 2000
All rights reserved.

Printed in Germany 1 2   4 5 6 7

Dedicated to Loredana Marchi (Foyer, Brussels),
for familiarizing me with intercultural praxis,
and, as both - theory and praxis - are equally important to me,
also to Prof. Dr. Eugène Roosens (Catholic University of Leuven),
for having introduced me to the interethnic theory.

(Johan Leman)

# TABLE OF CONTENTS

# Preface to the second revised edition

In many places around the world we find that population groups have difficulty in relating to and coping with the existing large-scale bureaucratic structures, and this comes in a time when business and especially financiers are seeking increasingly to organise their activities in a multinational and, if possible, intercontinental manner. Rationalisation and upscaling of both thinking and action are seen here as synonymous with the kind of economic and political approach that will enable the groups in question to ensure their place at the head of the competitive table in the next century.

This is not only the case in the European Union. Key leaders in other continents share the view that size, globalisation and rationalisation are the paradigms for successful future policy, as demonstrated by the current South African leadership in Africa, by Japanese and South-East Asian business leaders and by policy-makers in the United States.

In this same period of urgent upscaling, however, the world is also transmitting frequent and emotionally forceful messages that testify to an entirely opposite development. Ordinary people caught up in such overarching structures are seemingly unwilling or unable to follow in the wake of these rational thinkers and practitioners with their globalising tendencies. New brands of nationalism are popping up everywhere. On a more informal level, population groups within a single space - or what used to be considered a single space - are displaying increasing rivalry based on origin, history, the lack of a common 'founding myth' or differences in language or skin colour. Nationalist and ethnicity movements are taking on post-modern proportions.

For some time, social science literature has correctly described as 'ethnicity phenomena' such tokens of resistance against large conglomerations and steady globalisation, through which people proclaim, on the basis of their history or current shared similarities, that they are different from the 'others' living around or amongst them.

Ethnicity is the subject of this collection of studies. A good deal of attention has already been paid in the literature to this 'we-consciousness' based on a supposed common past that is not shared with one's neighbours. Two questions have not, however, been adequately addressed until now, both of which have some relevance to the trend towards globalisation that has marked the final decennia of the 20th century.

The first question is whether or not, in an era criss-crossed with processes of transnational migrations on a planetary scale, increasingly common *migration-*

*linked* ethnicities differ essentially from *traditional indigenous* ones?

Secondly, at a time when secularisation is a key feature of the globalisation and upscaling that have become paradigms for efficient future management, to what extent are ethnic counter-movements *sparked off, sustained and advanced by religious (and to a lesser extent linguistic) emblems and structures?*

A related consideration that could be raised is whether all these counter-movements, in which a heightened and narrowed 'we-consciousness' is created, are really as related to the past as their rhetoric often suggests? Is it not the case that many of them are actually more *future-oriented*, seeking to reposition a population group that, in its fragmentation, might otherwise miss the train to the future?

These complex questions will be discussed in this publication in an empirical, anthropological manner, by analysing in great detail specific situations that are representative of the most common settings for ethnicity.

Can ethnicity be divided into categories, each with a series of specific varieties? And are there, particularly in the case of indigenous ethnicity, matrices that implicate themselves through various historical modulations and remain in the background to be activated in certain circumstances in the present?

These questions are dealt with by means of our series of field studies. This research was conducted between 1990 and 1997 in a research unit at the Department of Social and Cultural Anthropology at the Catholic University of Leuven, now continued by MERIB (Migration and Ethnicity Research Institute Brussels) at the same department. In this research, Greet Van de Vijver and Christiane Stallaert focussed primarily on the second question concerning the creation modalities of indigenous ethnicity, Wen-Chin Chang and I studied a number of immigrant ethnicities, and Kathleen Ghequière focussed on a field where both, indigenous and immigrant ethnicities are at work in the creation of new meanings.

For the study of indigenous ethnicity, the fieldwork is situated on two ethnically sensitive places with a rich cultural past that have a lot in common but also differ sufficiently. They are the ethnic Romanians and Magyars from Transylvania, and the Spaniards and Spanish regionalists. In each case, it is determined how, in the present ethnic discussions, a social matrix is active, the seeds of which can be found centuries ago and this to such a degree that historiography permits a more than objective reconstruction deep into the past.

How completely different do the processes occur among the "immigrant ethnicities". Here it never comes to matrices. The dynamic of the processes never is of a sufficiently long duration. If true community formation occurs in a number of cases, it is based on originally indigenous ethnicities that have entered the country along with the immigrants (as is the case with the Suryoye from the Southeast of Turkey). In some cases the ultimate modeling of allochthonous (immigrant) communities or parts of them among the third and fourth generation have a strongly religious coloration also (as is the case with the muslim immigrants or other religious minority groups in Western Europe).

The contributions are a plea not to neglect the importance of history and of religions in the study of the most burning present-day ethnic subjects, even if every ethnic project has also as principle objective to deal with the future. They also join those authors who have abandoned the idea that it is possible to bring all forms of ethnicity under one, single category.

At the same time, the publication may also be considered to be an anthropologically supported plea to commence the study of history not just with the Enlightenment and Modernity but already many centuries earlier for a clear understanding of present social changes.

A final question that should be asked, however, is whether the concept of 'ethnicity', as described in the predominantly Western literature, is in fact always the most appropriate 'rationale' to denote the processes that occur from both an immigrant-ethnic and indigenous-ethnic point of view, particularly if these take place in a non-Western context. The contribution by Wen-Chin Chang on the Kuomintang (i.e. "Nationalist") Yunnanese Chinese in Northern Thailand, for instance, might cause the reader to ask wehether another reality is not at work; even though the author does not elaborate on this in her article another rationality may be at work, on the basis of a constantly re-modulating yin (female) - yang (male) structuralism that is much more fundamental, and hence much more relevant, than an external approach using Western ethnicity constructs might lead one to suspect. This inevitably raises the question - particularly where the author is discussing the socio-cultural resettlement of the KMT Chinese in northern Thailand and comparing the role of the military in the organisation of refugee villages against that of women - of how the men and women in question experience and interpret this emotionally and cognitively from within their own world view.

The ethnicity debate appears to be of only secondary importance, at least for the people involved, and it is questionable whether it would become an essential issue at some later stage either.

Perhaps 'ethnicity' is not always the most appropriate notion by which to identify in a Chinese reality phenomena that current anthropology would view as 'ethnic'.

*In comparison to the first edition, two subjects in particular are given extra attention in this revised edition in chapters 1, 2, and 7 (Leman): certain developments in the large cities that show how ethnicities are absorbed to a certain level by religions whereby the supra-ethnic religiosity can generate a number of modulators for social positioning in the allochthon communities and, consequently, the not unimportant place occupied by the cultural perception of the "otherness" in the instrumentalisation or not of ethnic traits.*

*In addition, Chang (Chapter 3), Van de Vijver (Chapter 5) and Stallaert (Chapter 6) have introduced some changes in this second edition.*

Prof. Dr. Johan Leman
Department of Social and Cultural Anthropology : MERIB (Migration and Ethnicity Research Institute Brussels), Catholic University of Leuven (Belgium), Director of the federal Center for Equal Opportunities and Opposition to Racism (Brussels)

# Chapter I:

# Introduction

Johan Leman

## 1. The topicality of ethnicity

The question we seek to answer in all the following chapters is what happens precisely when a group of people or an entire population group has always distinguished itself from its neighbours or suddenly begins to do so on the basis of external characteristics such as language, religion or other features *and* on the basis of a perceived history. Aramaic Christians from South-East Turkey (Suryoye) have distinguished themselves from other Christian groups, Muslims and Kurds for centuries. Many North African immigrants to Western Europe, however, suddenly become much more religious than they ever were in their native country.

How does this come about? What led up to it? Where is it leading? Is the process always the same? Does this correspond with a population group that simply considers itself self-sufficient ('we' against 'the rest of the world'), or is it aimed at one or two neighbouring peoples with the rest of the world ignored in the social debate? Is the process always as fundamental? Is it a regressive phenomenon in social organisation or does it help imbue people with a new dynamism with which to approach the future? Do some favoured emblems and structures feature more than others in the profiling of the group?

All of what we term 'ethnicity' can appear at times to be highly subjective and arbitrary in character - an artificial state that will not last. This might be suggested by the phenomenon of Italian-Americans or ethnic Swedish- or Polish-Americans who demand a lot of attention for a while. On the other hand, there are places in the world where former neighbours murder one another for their differences and where countries disintegrate. Grudges that have simmered for centuries can boil over for people who are still adolescents or young adults and for whom life had hitherto been entirely peaceful. One has only to look at the former Yugoslavia, Rwanda and some of the former Soviet Republics.

We might well ask in such situations whether the crux of the problem is genuinely the avowed bone of contention or whether this content is, in fact, secondary and the process actually derives from social antagonisms with entirely different causes. And if so, isn't there basically also some conception of 'otherness' at work, which brings us back to culture, not as "cultural stuff" (Barth 1969: 15) but as preconscious cultural attitude (result of education and of the orientation of social institutions)?

## 2. Rationale for choice of case studies

All of the above questions could be approached in a highly theoretical manner. The authors of this publication wanted, however, to tackle them in a different way. Situations were sought that were sufficiently manageable to be grasped in their full complexity, thereby allowing the nuances of religious and linguistic interference in the debate to be precisely identified. At the same time the particular situations also had to be sufficiently representative to allow generalised conclusions to be drawn. Comparison of the situations had to be able to lead spontaneously to the observance of similarities and differences. Finally, the proposed case studies required the potential to shed light on the prevailing ethnicity debate.

The first cluster of questions that the case studies had to illuminate naturally concerned the issue of whether everything identified as ethnicity by outsiders can in fact best be explained using that paradigm. It is similarly open to question whether religion and language helped construct ethnicity (or what might be perceived as such) in the same way in each continent. These findings are implicitly prompted e.g. by the discussion of the Kuomintang Yunnanese Chinese in northern Thailand (Chang).

The purpose of the adopted approach may be further clarified if the study of Chinese refugees is read in the light of the discussion that precedes it of the ethnicity of Mediterranean immigrants of the guest-worker type in Western Europe (Leman). Certain elements are detected in both situations - homesickness on the part of the first generation for the native region, the ties of the second generation with the place in which they were born and with their parents. However, the dissimilar nature of the migrations in the two cases - KMT Chinese in northern

Thailand and people of Mediterranean origin in Western Europe - and the impact of differing world views on specific assumptions, cause Chang to refer with regard to the KMT Chinese to a 'process of identifiying which bears both subjective and objective dimensions', without this resulting in the same structuring (almost 'logical') step-by-step ethnic phasing as among Mediterranean people of the guest-worker type in western Europe.

Whatever the case, a trend then seems to emerge regarding migration ethnicity, according to which the ethnic features of group formation amongst immigrants, whether of the 'forced' or 'voluntary' type, are primarily characterised by transience and are very often absorbed by elements of religious structuring. This is sometimes found in the first generation (in the form of pious religious fundamentalism) but is more emphatically apparent amongst the third generation - substantially more so in the case of Muslim immigrants than those belonging to the Chinese religion. The difference between religious absorption in the first generation and that in a third generation and further is that, in the former, it generally involves pious religious fundamentalism on a mono-ethnic basis (Leman 1998) while in the latter case, supra-ethnic religious coordinating processes are often operative (Scantlebury 1995; Leman 1999).

This does not prevent the incidence in immigration of forms of ethnicity that are not linked to migration. Aramaic Christians from South-East Turkey (Ghequière), for instance, had built up an intergroup relationship with the surrounding Muslims and Kurds centuries before their migration. It is questionable, however, whether these original relationships were already of an ethnic and antagonistic nature or whether they were purely social and religious, to which an ethnic tinge was later added during the immigration stage.

The quality and degree of ethnicity as defined in the literature are, therefore, fairly flexible in the context of what is known as 'migration ethnicity'. The three specific but generalisable migration situations (Mediterranean guest-worker emigration followed by chain migration, Yunnanese involuntary refugee migration, and the transition of a fairly isolated and small Aramaic population group from South-East Turkey to Western Europe) provide an effective basis for a thorough study of the nature of group formation and the processes of identification, and of the associated function of language and religion.

A second issue, which must again be clarified by means of case studies, relates to the rationale of indigenous ethnicity, which has the potential to cause the disintegration of countries and to spark all kinds of bloodbath, while in other cases appearing entirely superficial and arbitrary. Two important European settings for multi-ethnicity are analysed. The first is the account of Spanish ethnogenesis, which occupied such a dominant position throughout centuries of Spanish history and yet has culminated in far-reaching regionalism and several important nationalisms (Stallaert). The second is the situation in Transylvania (Rumania), where there is a strong rivalry between Rumanian and Hungarian minorities and, to a much lesser extent, the Rom gypsies who have been forced into an inferior social position and are not really involved on an interethnic level (Van de Vijver). Once again, the situation of the Aramaic Christians from South-East Turkey is interesting, but in this case primarily as far as the period before their migration is concerned.

In each of the three cases a socially and religiously antagonistic relationship between Christianity and Islam is important either at the beginning (Spain and Turkey) or at a somewhat later stage of their history (Transylvania - where such a relationship is less emphatic but still exists to some degree). It is evident on each occasion that the original matrix was not ethnic but religious in character. The three case studies illustrate once again how religion and language (and their interaction), going back this time to the pre-modern period and characterised by a matrix formation stretching over several centuries, constantly sustain the glowing embers from which the sparks of later interethnic conflicts can fly causing fires to break out today - centuries later.

It is interesting in this context to note that Edgar Morin pointed even out that the Islam made Europe and that Europe was only recognized as a reaction and a defense towards the Islam (Morin 1987: 35 and 37).

One might ask whether a particular ethnicity that is characteristic of society in the United States does not come over as even more 'artificial', 'created', 'open to manipulation' and 'transitory' (Hollinger 1995), in view of the fact that it has arisen largely from migration ethnicity (unless perhaps in the case of Afro-American and Hispanic groups).

## 3. Population groups studied

The following chapter focuses on the development of ethnicity as has occurred as a result of migration from Southern Europe, North Africa and Turkey to the north-west of Europe. Trade unions and churches have been obliged to adopt new positions towards these newcomers. To some extent, immigrants have brought their own religious institutions with them, especially the Muslims and some Orthodox Christian groups. Their children are socialised in Western values by the schools. What scope then remains for this second generation in terms of ethnic expression? And how have their own children further developed their family and social life? These issues are examined with respect to the different subgroups at various moments in the postwar migration process with a view to identifying common characteristics.

In a related yet contrasting development, an entirely different type of migration - that of the forced type - has been experienced by Nationalist Chinese since the Communist seizure of power in China. This is not a form of labour migration, nor has it given rise to genuine 'chain' mechanisms. It has occurred, furthermore, in a similar religious but varying linguistic setting. This offers a perfect opportunity to place the ethnicity issue as formulated in the context of migration in its proper perspective. Although no migration can serve as a perfect model for others, there are undoubtedly certain similarities between these specific 'small-scale' Chinese migrations and other refugee situations elsewhere in the world.

The two chapters on migration are linked to the two on indigenous interethnicity by a chapter on a small but very interesting minority group (the Aramaic or Suryoye people) from South-East Turkey which, after a long history of social and religious positioning with respect to other groups in Turkey, has emigrated almost in its entirety to the West in the final decades of the 20th century (U.S.A, Germany, Sweden, The Netherlands, Belgium...). In addition to internal Christian positioning, this development is patently based on a confrontation between Christianity and Islam, with an Aramaic-Kurdish relationship added for good measure. It is this historically evolved matrix that has come back into play in the West, this time via processes that have predominantly to do with migration ethnicity.

As far as chapters 2, 3 and 4 are concerned, an interesting discussion naturally arises - which we will touch on here for a moment - as to what proportion of geographical movements of human groups may be identified as 'migrations' and what explanatory model may be applied most effectively in each case to explain such migrations whenever they occur? The 'push-pull' model predominates in post-war western literature, which has set out primarily to analyse migrations of the guest-worker type. We might well ask why western social scientists were unwilling to identify earlier colonial movements simply as migration flows, while being content to do so in the case of the subsequent displacement of inhabitants of former colonies in the context of guest-worker movements (Nwolisa-Okanga 1999: 71)?

Many refugee flows can also be identified in part as migration movements. Some authors (e.g. Kunz 1973) stress the push element in what they see as involuntary migrations.

Kunz characterises refugee movements as 'kinetic' (Kunz 1973: 131). Although it is true that refugee flows are influenced by shifting military and international relations in the region in which they occur, the case of the KMT Chinese shows that refugees are not always the plaything of these relations and that they also attempt in part to make their own choices.

Specific internal dynamics, forms of leadership, resettlement and so on certainly develop within refugee flows when proper organisation can begin.

It is interesting to note that within every type of migration, both voluntary and involuntary, people develop their own creativity - to some degree at least - and attempt to dermine and achieve their own options as quickly as possible. The difference lies in the fact that the linear phasing via a first, then a second and third generation that is so frequently encountered in the case of guest-worker migration is subject to much more complex processes in the case of involuntary migrations. Second-generation KMT Chinese, for instance, with parents who came to northern Thailand from Yunnan via Burma, often become first-generation migrants themselves, having migrated to Taiwan.

These variations are naturally important if a proper understanding is to be achieved of what may be considered a process within migration ethnicity, in addition, of course, to the issue of whether or not ethnic tensions already existed in the region of origin (as was the case with the Suryoye in south-eastern Turkey).

Naturally, the complex varied reality of the migrations is not limited to voluntary migrations of the guest-worker type and involuntary or forced refugee migrations. Initially more of an American phenomenon, the transnationalism whereby a new field is established of a country of origin and host country that present themselves as mutually complementary and whereby the continuous going to and from is a self-evident reality (Guarnizo 1994) is gradually also becoming a fact for population groups in Europe at the end of the twentieth century (Van Broeck 1999). Our study, however, does not go into this phenomenon.

The fifth chapter takes us to Transylvania on the periphery of the former Ottoman Empire. The element of Islam versus Christianity is less emphatic here than in the case of South-East Turkey, as the principal rivalry (from the religious point of view at least) is between Orthodox Christians (ethnic Rumanians) versus Catholics (ethnic Hungarians). In the background, however, both sides seek to draw some of their ideological legitimacy through the greater perceived resistance they once offered to the advance of Islam in the West. As with the Suryoye in South-East Turkey, there is a strong interaction amongst both the ethnic Rumanians and the ethnic Hungarians between religion and language.

The ethnicity debate cannot, however, be reduced to the actions and positions adopted by minority groups, be they immigrant or indigenous. The identity of entire nations can also be tested on the basis of this paradigm. This is done in our publication by means of a thorough and detailed study of the origin and growth of Spain's identity which was bound almost inherently to lead to a proliferation of regional subidentities of the same kind of purity. The authors are living in Belgium, one of Europe's countries where the ethnicity debate frequently takes very irrational proportions. I wonder if the so-called peaceful Belgian solutions for the ethnic problems, at each stage of the ethnic debate, are not principally due to the absence of any deep antagonistic religious matrix in pre-modern times, and the focussing on only language issues, which makes it different from situations in Northern Ireland and even Spain. The last case study rounds off the range of possible situations.

#### 4. Migration and indigenous ethnicity; ethnicity and culture

The final chapter deals with the question, based on existing anthropological literature, of what are really the most important distinctions between a migration ethnicity and an indigenous one. What are the similarities and what are the differences? The structure that emerges from the case studies themselves is probably the best guarantee of the clearness of the conclusions.

Migration ethnicity focuses on the past, albeit the near past (at most, three generations deep). Indigenous ethnicity focuses on boundary delimitation with respect to the other – preferably the next-door neighbour, and uses the past, which is situated in long-past centuries, to legitimate the boundary and the antagonism.

Barth has stressed the 'boundary' in the ethnicity debate because he primarily wanted to shed light on the social antagonism and the instrumentalism of the cultural stuff subordinated to it. The question is, however, not only whether thereby attention to the origin (and to the historical dimension) remains under-emphasised but also whether the meaning of culture in the ethnicity debate did not remain too restricted to a materiality to be instrumentalised. Correctly, Roosens points out that "the origin of a group, expressed by means of the family metaphor and involving popular genealogy" (Roosens 1994: 100) is at the origin of the ethnicity. One can probably go a step further. Is not the filling in of the family metaphor specific for a particular group – and consequently the accompanying pre-reflexive sensing of 'otherness' as attributed to the others who are not included in one's own group by the family metaphor, fundamental for the antagonistic disposition or not of the ethnicity – that leads to situating the question of culture-based or boundary-based ethnicity at a deeper level than is the case with Barth (cf. Bafekr & Leman 1999)?

Our study is not directed to this last question, even though it is implicitly present in the approach of Chang (Chapter 3) and Stallaert (Chapter 6). It is primarily the question of the distinction between migration ethnicity and indigenous ethnicity and of the place of the religion and the language that prevail. And it is from the analyses themselves that an answer to this must gradually emerge.

# Chapter II:

## Mediterranean immigrant ethnicities

**Johan Leman**

My findings about immigrant ethnicities are based on my own fieldwork, which began with a study of Sicilian allochthonous people living in Brussels between 1974 and 1980, continued by examining a small Sicilian colony in Casablanca, Morocco in 1979 and was supplemented between 1981 and 1989 by research among Moroccan and Turkish allochthonous people living in Brussels (1982, 1987, 1990, 1991). New ethnografic research on interethnicity in metropolitan situations, especially in Brussels (1999a, 1999b) is added to this study. In reference to the post-war Southern Italian immigrants, within the context of the European Union, they are now, in the 1990s, no longer regarded as immigrants (as was the case until the late 1970s), but have acquired a status that links them closely to the autochthonous population, or are even completely assimilated with the indigenous population. In Belgium, for example, the son of a former immigrant worker from Italy became Deputy Prime Minister at the end of 1994 and many other second-generation Italians have taken up important positions within the administration or in trade unions. It is somewhat otherwise for the non-EU residents. Moreover, the metropolitan processes partly manifest a dynamic of their own.

## 1. Do 'ethnic networks' exist among first-generation Mediterranean immigrants?

### 1.1. *Fragmentary spontaneous networks as offshoots from the past*

Among first-generation Sicilian, Moroccan and Turkish allochthons in Belgium a highly specific and recurring profile is evident: the women concentrate on running the household and are dependent for their social life on other women in their immediate environment or in their extended family. These are usually minor relationships, which can, however, be characterized by some degree of intensity. For financial reasons some women also look for a job, but employment does not really offer them a means of building up a network of relationships outside working hours.

Among Mediterranean men, the emphasis on 'friends' and on other men, by means of which they develop their social identity, is greater than among the women, and needs to be expressed publicly - and in some people's eyes ostentatiously. As a result the spontaneous formation of networks in bars, cafes and sports clubs is more visible and gives a neighborhood a look that is strongly influenced by social and cultural elements of the region of origin.

This 'ethnic' look is reinforced by the development of an 'ethnic'-looking immigrant middle class and, in the case of neighborhoods with an allochthonous Islamic population, by the conversion of workshops or larger houses into small mosques targeted on people from specific regions of origin.

The process described here is spontaneous network formation, which provides people who find themselves in a new situation with some continuity with the life they knew in their region of origin without them being confronted with explicit ethnic diacritical markers that represent something different from the life they once led in their region of origin. If we concur with the analysis criteria developed by Don Handelman (1977), it cannot be denied that this can lead to a series of de facto "ethnic ascriptions" and can also give rise to de facto "interaction along ethnic lines". What is involved here, however, is certainly not prescribed behavior, which means that many exceptions are possible and that this behavior can change considerably over time.

1.2.    *The ethnicity-reducing character of traditional 'establishment' associations*

The social life of men can acquire a formal basis when they join associations that are affiliated with the larger trade unions. Here again it is not so much the job itself that forms the starting point for building a fabric of relationships, except in the case of the miners' culture (which came to an end in Western Europe in the late

1960s), but alternatively an association that is an exponent of trade unionism. Both cases, i.e. the miners' lives (cf. more general account in Nash 1979) and associations affiliated with a trade union, do involve network formation and even an organizational structure that leads to the formation of ingroups and outgroups. However, ethnic markers, used to differentiating on the basis of origin from a specific "foreign" region, play no part or are only of very minor importance, for example in the initial recruitment stage.

Religion can also form a basis for creating networks. One of the first frameworks imported from the home country that homes in on the community life of the immigrants is established by providers of religious services. Along with the immigrants from traditionally Catholic countries like Italy and Spain came many priests and nuns who organized worship in the immigrants' own language and saw to the important religious ceremonies (baptism, confirmation, solemn communion and, particularly, marriage), once again in the language and according to the cultural traditions of their congregation.

Among the Moroccan and Turkish Muslims something similar occurred later on. However, in the case of Islam, as practiced in a non-Islamic society, there is an additional element of support for social diversity, via some of the organizational principles that are considered to be the essence of Islam: the collective duty to observe the annual Ramadan and, to a lesser extent, the exhortation to say ritual prayers in the mosque on Friday afternoons, particularly during Ramadan. The mosque and Ramadan are unquestionably among the public markers that from the very beginning of immigration lend themselves the most objectively to ethnic differentiation. It is noteworthy, however, that both markers, with respect to both first-generation Islamic allochthons and non-Islamic autochthons, when they are presented as being "problematic", are not substantiated by ethnic arguments. There may be mutual discontent based on social or religious arguments (e.g., disruption of street life and the preaching of the imams, respectively).

As the proportion of second-generation immigrants increases, what usually happens in Western Europe is a gradual merging of the allochthonous religious frameworks with those of the host country (in the case of the Catholics) or with a new framework, first perceived as allochtonous religiosity, that gradually develops in the host country (in the case of the Muslims).

## 1.3. The absorption of ethnicity by fundamentalist religions

One process that, as we have just noted, can interfere with the ethno-religious network formation among first-generation immigrants is pietistic and fundamentalist in nature. In this process, an existing institutionalized fundamentalist religious model presents itself to immigrants who, for social or economic reasons (e.g., grave uncertainty about the standards to be adopted in social intercourse, problems in bringing up their children, or unemployment and loss of status of the husband), are experiencing a decline in standards or a shift in roles within the context of the allocation of tasks or status within the family. By joining a fundamentalist religious group with strictly prescribed traditional family values and a high degree of internal social control, the cohesion of the family can be restored, at least temporarily and at the parental level. In such fundamentalist groups, which present themselves as a confirmation of cultural continuity, attention is given to the language of origin, which is routinely used for the meetings. Broadly speaking, this certainly provides some explanation for the relative success of religious movements like the Jehovah's Witnesses among first-generation immigrants from Southern Europe in the 60ies and 70ies (Leman 1979a).

Similar movements may be perceived among the many allochthonous religious movements, as is the case with the Milli Görüs (National Vision) among Turkish Islamic immigrants, and the Jama'at at Tabligh (Society for the Mission) among Islamic immigrants in Western Europe.

However, a same phenomenon of enforced fundamentalist religious devotion can occur in middleclass groups (and younger intellectuals) who have to orient themselves in periodes of fast social changes.

To outsiders, these kinds of movements have a strong ethno-religious profile, but the participants themselves do not perceive such an ethnic element and are completely absorbed by their religious identification.

## 2. Fragments of ethno-cultural construction among second-generation immigrants

2.1. *Focus on the host country and particularly on the family in which they were raised*

Studies of second-generation immigrants have shown that these groups predominantly focus on the host country, as a result of their education (Leman 1979b; Roosens 1989 and 1995).

They are linked to their culture of origin by their parents and grandparents as well as by those elements that are an integral part of their domestic family culture, in which they are immersed and to which they are exposed until such time as they are of school age. Thereafter they depend on the school for their social integration into public life, and even though a great many bridging elements to their culture of origin and to their domestic situation can be incorporated, this does not alter the fact that for some considerable time the dominant social values they acquire and the way in which they behave, think and feel will be determined by what society offers via school, street life and the peer group (Leman 1979b).

In fact, a process of continuous erosion of their culture of origin has started, yet at the same time, of course, a process of continuous assimilation of information from the popular culture of the host country is also under way, as is the case for autochthonous young people.

The contact that is maintained from time to time with the country of origin cannot reverse this trend, with the result that the country of origin is increasingly regarded as "foreign" and that the second-generation immigrants themselves are treated as "foreigners" when they visit there during the holidays.

The same authors who stress this predominant focus on the host country and invariably demonstrate the erosion of the culture of origin also point to the inconsistency of this focus and to elements that seem to indicate a new link with the region of origin. "The grandparents come to serve as a symbol of continuity, offering an anchor for the sense of ethnic identity" (Epstein 1978: 111). "Allochthonous languages may stay alive and so may elements of imported religions and cultures. Symbolic ethnicity may flourish..." (Roosens 1995: 20).

I myself talked about "fragmenting creativity" (Leman 1987: 102-123) and "at most only an emotional relationship to the region of origin" (p. 123), which basically stemmed from childhood and from domestic life with their parents and immediate family.

While it is true that, for second-generation immigrants, focussing on the host country implies focussing on the popular culture of the host country in its most publicly visible form, at the same time it also means focussing on the family that has brought them up, including their parents and grandparents.

Undoubtedly the "emotional relationship" seeks to express itself. And although there are social and religious factors that can encourage or help to give expression to it, this does not invalidate the basic focus on the host country where one is socialized.

In her fieldwork among KMT Yunnanese Chinese minorities in refugee villages in the Chiang Mai and Chiang Rai provinces of Northern Thailand, Wen-Chin Chang points out that many young second-generation immigrants emigrate for the purposes of secondary education and work to Taiwan, a country to which they have always had emotional ties due to their political affiliation with the KMT government there. This confronts us with a situation that is very different from that in Western Europe and warns us that we must avoid excessive generalizations in the discussion of immigrant ethnicities.

However, although the refugee villages of Northern Thailand are mainly associated with traumatic experiences for these second-generation immigrants and although Taiwan is the country to which they are drawn, many still say "that they don't feel they are Taiwanese when they are in Taiwan, and they don't feel they are Thai when they are in Thailand. They grew up in these refugee villages of Northern Thailand. Their homes have been there" (Chang 1996). The place where one grows up and, in particular, the family one comes from, is and will always be an emotional anchor.

The question is, therefore, exactly what message has to be deciphered from phenomena of symbolic ethnicity, where these occur among second-generation immigrants. Does this not often concern the externalization of an emotional bond with the culture in which one has been raised as a child within the family?

## 2.2. *Symbolic markers without community implications*

How should the practice of wearing a headdress, as a symbolic marker, be interpreted in the case of an Islamic schoolgirl in Western Europe who is acting of her own free will and not under any pressure from her father? In doing so, does she want to indicate that she belongs to a group that wants to react against her fellow pupils or against the school, or is it her intention to establish a group of pupils around this symbolic act? Does she want to indicate that she is predominantly focussed on her culture of origin or on the religion of her parents or grandparents and that at the same time she wants to react against the popular values of society? In actual fact these are often the interpretations that non-Islamic receivers of the message place on her action, which can account for the resentment of principals and teachers.

It might well be the case, of course, that these factors are taken into consideration by some imams who speak to fathers on this subject. The question then arises what impact these preachers have on fathers and how long it can be sustained. The case we have in mind, however, is a strictly personal initiative, involving a personal construction by a young second-generation immigrant by means of an easy to use religious symbol. This kind of symbolism does not require full ethnic interpretation and can be seen as simply a personal mark of respect for an origin that a woman, temporarily or otherwise, wishes to include as part of her social identity.

In the same sense, someone can publicly call himself Islamic and can explicitly claim this identity for himself, even though he has never shown any interest previously and his conversion to Islam is not accompanied by a desire to explore the religion in depth or by any great interest in its practice.

Is this ethnicity? It seems more accurate to speak of a construction by means of symbolic markers that are temporarily or more permanently integrated into the social identity of a person without being accompanied by the formation of a community based on these markers. The ethnic (and possibly also the religious) dimension of this kind of ethno-cultural construction is therefore very limited, despite the social and ethnic overinterpretation that is usually placed on such events, especially by outsiders. Naturally this type of person can be integrated into a wider network, as already discussed in the case of first-generation immigrants.

Finally, one special form of ethnicity that can occur among second-generation immigrants is the so-called "ethnic riot" of young people in some working-class areas of large cities, as happened at the end of the 80ies and the beginning of the 90ies in France, United Kingdom and Belgium.

Here too, from an ethnic point of view, it is essentially all about symbolism. This is shown by the fact that place, time and objects of aggression usually correspond to a fixed pattern. Territory is at the heart of an allochthonous neighborhood, and as evening approaches, just at the moment when the hustle and bustle of the day is dying down, aggression is directed at the police, who represent society as ideal opponents and, on the other hand, at the better class of shops in the area.

Whereas in the case of individual construction with symbolic markers, it is mainly the emotional involvement of the young people in their foreign origins that is exploited and no reference to a wider group is evident, this element of involvement in the past is completely absent in the case of mass riots and their ethnic character is limited to an ethnic mass antagonism based purely on frustration. Territory - which is actually the most recognizable expression of a genuine community - and which effectively lies at the heart of the mobilization, functions merely as a symbol for the occasion that immediately disintegrates when the emotionality of the mobilization passes its peak (Leman 1994). Here too essential elements are missing that would enable us to speak of full-fledged ethnicity.

### 3. Other forms of "immigrant ethnicity" among later generations?

Among the allochthons in Belgium who originate from Southern Europe no real "ethnic associations", in the sense of Don Handelman's "goal-oriented corporate organizations", have yet been formed among later generations, let alone any "communities" based on territory. This is probably partially because such formation in the context of immigration presupposes the existence of more deeply rooted, inherited matrices that regulate the mutual perceptions between groups.

When one has immigrants who emigrate to a country of their own free will and with a country that offers genuine opportunities to newcomers to enable them to be integrated into their new homeland, forms of "immigrant ethnicity" will indeed occur, as described above. However, this does not normally lead to separate communities that want to have sole power to determine their own internal social intercourse and that thus ultimately demand clearly defined territory for this purpose. To put it another way, "immigrant ethnicity" does not normally lead to nationalist movements.

What does in fact happen is that immigrants from a particular background become integrated to very different degrees, with the possibilities ranging from minimal multiculturalism (where a group of people is very highly concentrated in a particular neighborhood and looks to the ingroup for social intercourse) through various intermediate forms of integration where groups are involved with and live alongside people from a different background while retaining fragments of their own cultural identity to far-reaching assimilation. This process, which already starts among the first-generation immigrants, albeit on a very limited scale, continues with each successive generation.

In addition to specific forms of ethno-cultural construction, which can also be found among third-generation immigrants, religion can offer a more permanent basis for specific organic network formation. This is associated with ethnic diversity, so long as this religion continues to attract mainly people of recognizably allochthonous origin among the congregation.

The Sicilians studied as part of my fieldwork in Casablanca (Morocco) (Leman 1982: 447-451; Leman 1987: 127-130) offer a good example of this. Although they were absorbed as a group into the category of Europeans (along with the French and the Spanish), who in turn differentiated themselves from all the other inhabitants along Islamic-Christianity lines, nevertheless they identified themselves as Sicilians during one particular religious festival, in honor of the Madonna of Trapani, for one day a year.

It may also be presumed that among later generations of allochthons in Western Europe, the religious institutional factor in the case of the Muslims (and in other countries also the Hindus) will set out a limited set of markers around which community formation will take place with ethnic connotations. Some of these allochthons will organize themselves on a purely internal basis as regards a limited number of social relations. This may range from a minimum (i.e. fulfilling religious or social duties) to a maximum (where everything is arranged internally as far as possible, from education, school to marriage). Where it is legally possible to establish Islamic schools, this of course provides a strong supporting system for specific ethno-religious community building. Normally speaking, such an initiative will be taken by first-generation allochthons (Dwyer and Meyer 1996).

Our "immigrant ethnicity" approach has so far remained abstract in the sense that the three generations have been kept apart. This does not of course correspond to the complex reality we witness today. Where ethnic, or more likely mainly ethno-religious community formation takes place, the three generations are generally all mixed together. This means for example, that network formation in the extension of the region of origin, with particular attention given to ethno-religious markers and agreements made within the ingroup concerning matters of social intercourse, possibly even including forms of endogamy - albeit not obligatory - encompasses an entire community of one ethnic type or a neighborhood in which several communities (e.g. Moroccans, Turks and a smaller Pakistani and a smaller Sub-Saharan network) live alongside one another. Such a result is gradually taking shape in Belgium and elsewhere in continental Europe.

In times of economic crisis, while class identification declines, this community aspect becomes stronger.

## 4. Possible interference of "indigenous ethnicity"

A second reason why our "immigrant ethnicity" approach remains somewhat abstract is that in many cases there can be a mingling with "indigenous ethnicity". Brussels already offers two clear examples of "non-immigrant ethnicity" within immigration situations. The two examples are highly instructive, have a great deal to say about the many forms that ethnicity can adopt in immigration, and consequently deserve some attention.

The first example concerns the situation of the undocumented Polish immigrants from Podlasie (Northeast Poland).

The features that characterize the life of an undocumented immigrant who emigrates with a view to finding illegal work can be summarized as follows: as an immigrant he focusses on work, money and a good relationship with his employer. The administration in the host country does not function at all as an integrating factor. Only a minimum amount is invested in housing. Recreation and entertainment is necessary after a while, but is arranged within the ingroup (Leman 1995).

In the case of undocumented Latin-American immigrants in Brussels, they are far removed from their country of origin, so that regular contact is rare. Networks are formed through recreation and assume the form described above in relation to first-generation immigrants, albeit limited to the sphere of recreation.

The situation is very different for the undocumented Polish immigrants because of the proximity of Brussels to Podlasie. Every week buses depart from both places and visitors regularly travel back and forth. Mentally and emotionally, the undocumented Polish immigrants never actually leave Podlasie. They are "present" in Brussels but do not "live" there. Every weekend the Poland that these undocumented people left behind is recreated through Polish Catholic religious worship. This takes place via cassettes containing Polish hymns, which are played during the service, and through the sermons given by a Polish priest, who addresses the Polish congregation, instilling in them a feeling of great self-worth with regard to the city where they have come to seek work and to Western Europe in general. Everyone who attends Mass leaves Brussels behind for a while and finds himself mentally and emotionally back in Poland.

It is not the Polish priests themselves who are the ethno-religious leaders but rather the institution of the Polish Church. The priests act like border guards, protecting Polish ethno-religious boundaries. This is not "immigrant ethnicity" but rather pure autochthonous Polish ethnicity. In that sense it is not surprising that undocumented Polish immigrants are indeed effectively "present" in Brussels but continue to "live" in Poland.
The same "autochthonous ethnicity" is found among undocumented Filipino immigrants in Brussels (Leman 1997).

The second example concerns the Christian Aramaic refugee community (i.e. the Suryoye) from Southeast Turkey. Although there is no doubt that processes are under way among these people in Brussels that can be described as "immigrant ethnicity", nevertheless it appears that they are involved in a relationship with the Islamic allochthons, which is just as fundamental and dates back to a matrix that had existed for many centuries in the region of origin.

Following the same train of thought, it may be interesting to explore to what extent a similar historical matrix plays a part in forming the attitudes of Spanish immigrants towards Moroccan immigrants. Undoubtedly this will take place in a less obtrusive manner than in the case of the Christian Aramaics, in view of the more recent traumatic experiences of the latter, but it will certainly intervene. This, however, is not "immigrant" ethnicity.

## 5.  Supra-ethnic processes

Subgroups from the various ethnic communities can, in turn, join together in coordinating religious communities in the multiethnic metropolitan situation. Such a supra-ethnic religiosity can be of a very different nature (Leman 1999a). It can concern religious systems that offer modules through which people from very divergent migrant communities can create for themselves the same social identity and whereby the believers can be presented a social 'model'. Thus, Pentecostal churches can be modulating for Bulgarian, Romanian, and Bosnian gypsy migrants, and Jehovah's Witnesses for Italian, Spanish, as well as Portuguese first-generation newcomers.   And sub-Saharan Africans can find the same communality in their 'new-era religions'.

These processes interfere with the differentiated ethnicity in metropolitan settings that we have already discussed above.

## 6.  Concluding remarks

How might we define "Mediterranean immigrant ethnicities"?  Obviously there are many possibilities.  Nearly always it involves seeking a link with a previous generation, and even two till three generations back. Nearly always there is also a feeling of "we". However, it is usually a question of the persons concerned facing the future in a less familiar present-day. And in a certain sense this may be more important than dwelling on the past.

In both cases the second generation, which clearly sees itself as transitional, presents a somewhat different profile.

In practice, however, the purely ethnic quality of a group's position does not appear to be so obvious, and the network that is interpreted as ethnic is actually either of a religious nature or an objective but fragmentary and modified continuation of a previous life in the region of origin, or a combination of the two interwoven with a few ethno-symbolic markers.

Our discussion of the "immigrant ethnicities" in the context of voluntary Mediterranean immigrations shows that, in the first generation, the clearest ethnic-based networks are provided by religion. However, such networks, if they become fundamentalist ones, are often ethnic only for outsiders because people involved do not experience them as such but identify with their religion.

In the second generation, a symbolic ethnicity appears primarily to give expression to an emotional bond that continues with the family in which one has been raised while, in addition, a drive for social promotion leads to far-reaching assimilation with the dominant culture (in casu generally the host country).

In the third generation, it is then primarily a potential community formation on the basis of a minority religion (see Jehovah's Witnesses) (Leman 1998) or of an originally allochthonous religion (see islam) (Gitmez and Wilpert 1987; Joly 1987; Leman 1996) that can continue to lead to ethnic profiling. However, the same religiosity can, when it recruits from different ethnic communities, give rise to processes of a supra-ethnic nature whereby people from different minority groups derive their social positioning in whole or in part from specific religious orientations pointing in different directions (Leman 1999a).

Of course, the generations, in the course of time, occur together in the immigrant communities, which means that the individual profiles influence each other.

Characteristic of "Mediterranean immigrant ethnicity" is that it does not really lead to the formation of a community based on territory and operated in accordance with ethnic interactions. Rather, it is fragmentary and less absorbing in its realization than might be expected of the process of ethnic community formation.

It must also be pointed out that a large range of intermediary forms can occur between the ideal type of purely voluntary immigration as is the case with the Mediterraneans and that of unvoluntary immigration, as is shown by the complex case of the KMT Yunnanese Chinese in Southeast Asia.

Where immigration involves more profound elements, in the sense of more deeply-rooted matrices in which ethnic attitudes are formed, we can no longer talk about "immigrant ethnicity". Instead, we must concern ourselves with "indigenous ethnicity", imported by the immigrants into their new social setting, upon which complementary "immigrant ethnicity" processes then become operative (see the Suryoye).

Subsequent articles in this publication will explore a case of unvoluntary or forced immigration, a case of immigrant ethnicity based on deeply-rooted historical matrices and some cases of indigenous ethnicity in greater depth.

# Chapter III:

# The Kuomintang Yunnanese Chinese of Northern Thailand

**Wen-Chin Chang**

## Introduction

Ethnic Chinese in Thailand have been a focus of sociological and anthropological studies for several decades. However most studies only examine the Chinese immigrants who came from the coastal provinces of southeast China to Thailand by the sea route and settled mostly in Thai urban areas. The Yunnanese Chinese who fled their hometowns to Burma and then northern Thailand carried out their migration overland. In contrast to the majority of ethnic Chinese who are concentrated in Thai cities and engage in trade, the first generation Yunnanese Chinese settled in self-founded villages which are often known as the KMT villages (Chang 1999: 1). Their migration had a complex military background related to the Republic of China in Taiwan and other political entities involved in the 1950s and 1960s. In this article, the author would like to discuss their migration, resettlement and ethnic identification. Each section will contain ethnographic information as well as theoretical analysis.

## 1 Involuntary migration from Yunnan

### 1.1 *Historical Background*

After the Chinese Communists took over the last province – Yunnan - from the hands of the Chiang Kai-Shek government in late 1949, most of the KMT[1] troops of the province could not be evacuated to Taiwan in time. They tried to withdraw to the southern neighboring countries -Vietnam, Laos and Burma. But a great number were defeated by the Communists before they could cross the border and reach the hoped destinations. The number that arrived in Burma was only about 3,000 in early 1950 according to the record of the Taiwanese government (Ministry of Defense, Taiwan 1964: 10, 11, 18). These remnants rejoined together and established their base in the area of Tachileik, a border town in one of the Shan states, Kentung. They tried to absorb other remnants which arrived later and also to recruit new members from civilian refugees. Meanwhile, they attempted to restore communications with the Chiang government that had withdrawn to Taiwan. Their hope was to recover their forces in Burma and fight back to their homeland as soon as possible. Supplies were provided by local Chinese immigrants, especially Yunnanese Muslim.

Their stay and activities irritated the Burmese government. The latter launched the first campaign against the KMT in June 1950[2]. The KMT were forced to move out of Tachileik. But they quickly reestablished another base in Mong Hsat, which was about 80 miles southwest of Kengtung town. It had a special tactical environment and became the headquarters of the KMT troops in Burma until the first evacuation in 1953-1954.

In August 1950, General Li Mi came from Taiwan to reorganize these troops and they were named "Yunnan Anti-Communist National Salvation Army" (ibid. : 287). The army expanded quickly by recruiting continuous inflows of Yunnanese refugees, earlier Chinese immigrants and local ethnic minorities. Several other bases were founded. The total number increased to 14,000 by the end of 1951 (ibid. : 17) and 16,068 in December 1953 (ibid. : form 6).

Informants said that after arriving in Burma, they had no other better choice than to join the KMT guerrilla troops which could give them food to eat and the hope to fight back to their homeland. There were wide disparities among the troops in terms of their capacities and resources. "Once you had a few men following you, you were a small leader," confirmed several informants. Within the area of the headquarters, military discipline was maintained, but exploitation happened in some other areas from time to time, such as forcible recruitment, collection of taxes and food, and ill-treatment of women through forced marriages. Nonetheless, informants emphasized that there had also been troops welcomed by local villagers. They traded with the indigenous people fairly and were well restrained by their leaders. In addition, the Burmese Army represented a foreign army of occupation to the local minorities (Yawnghwe 1990: 112).

Before the first evacuation to Taiwan in 1953-1954, the KMT guerrillas had a high morale. They believed they would soon fight back to China and rescue their compatriots who were suffering from communist torture. The guerrillas were under the direct command of the Chiang Kai-Shek government in Taiwan. The government was planning to recover China by advancing to the southeast coast of the mainland, and meanwhile the guerrillas could contain the communist forces from the south by crossing the Sino-Burmese border. On 5 January 1951, Chiang sent a telegram to the guerrillas. He told them:

> The past two years were the darkest period of our National Chinese and it was also the time for hard struggle for our National Chinese. The dark period has now begun to transit into a bright period.... all of you have been able to stick to your firm determination to...have a life and death struggle with a great number of traitors and bandits.... Your revolutionary spirit of unyielding and unceasingly fighting though suffering defeat after defeat will go down to the glorious history of the Chinese nation with praise and tears and also to point out the life line that leads to the road of existence and freedom, to the compatriots of the whole Chinese nation.... (Ministry of Information, the Union of Burma 1953: 181)

On 5 October 1951, the Yunnan Anti-Communist University was founded in Mong Hsat. Under the guise of an university, it functioned as a military training base, offering courses from a few weeks to a few months. At the beginning of the first training term, five military instructors and many other political staff officers were sent from Taiwan (T'an 1984: 98). Before taking the training courses, soldiers had to take the oath:

> With my conscience, I swear by Heaven and the portrait of our founding father [Sun Yat-Sen] that I vow to advocate the central government, obey orders of President Chiang, observe the Three Principles of the People, to fight to the end for our nationalist revolution.... (ibid. : 5)

Various constructions were completed: an airport in Mong Hsat was followed a few years later by an airstrip in Mong Pa Liao where airplanes with supplies from Taiwan could land , a dam in Mong Hsat for irrigation, a road from Bang Ba Chian to northern Thailand from where many supplies also came, and so on (ibid. : 101, 134, 164). These KMT guerrillas were on their sacred mission of anti-communism. Their bases spread over the triangular area on the east of the Salween River by mid 1952. It was adjoined to China in the north, to Laos in the east and to Thailand in the south.

The KMT also received supplies from the US whose major political policy was anti-communism during the cold-war period. The US considered the KMT guerrillas in Burma a useful force to prevent communist China from developing its influence southwards. While the Korean War was going on in 1951, the US asked the KMT to enter Yunnan to contain the Chinese Communists from the south. The KMT undertook several guerrilla wars back in Yunnan during their stay in Burma. They delivered propaganda and incited civilians to join them, but each time they were defeated by the Communists and had to flee to Burma again.

The Burmese government was very worried about the quick expansion of the KMT troops and their military activities. The Union of Burma was a newly founded state which had communist China on its north and the American supported Thailand on its south. The Burmese government tried to maintain a neutral policy between these two ideological blocs. It was afraid that communist China would invade Burma to fight these KMT guerrillas. In addition, the cooperation between some ethnic rebels and the KMT guerrillas was intolerable to the Burmese government. It was thus determined to expel these foreign forces from its country.

The Burmese government launched a series of campaigns to fight the KMT, but was unable to defeat them. It then sought help from the US government to pressure the Chiang Kai-Shek government to evacuate these troops, but that too yielded no result (Young 1970: 81-82). It finally filed an appeal in the UN on 25 March 1953, accusing the KMT guerrillas of being under direct command of the Chiang Kai-Shek government and of intended aggression against its national security and territorial integrity (Ministry of Information, the Union of Burma

1953). Discussions and debates were held. Taiwan denied its direct command over the KMT stragglers in Burma and insisted that it had no responsibility for them. It also argued that these Chinese guerrillas were staying in territory which had not been clearly demarcated between China and Burma (ibid. : 46,74; Young 1970: 105-108). On 23 April 1953, a UN resolution was reached. It condemned the presence of these "foreign forces" in Burma and required them to be disarmed and imprisoned or evacuated from Burma (Ministry of Defense, Taiwan 1964: 364). A four nation military committee was then set up to discuss the matter of evacuation. The committee members included representatives from the US, Taiwan, Burma and Thailand. Among the KMT troops, some were pro evacuation, but most were against it. Long discussions dragged on in the committee. The first phase of evacuation could not be carried out until November 1953. The evacuation was finished in May 1954. There were 6,500 evacuees to Taiwan, including both soldiers and civilians (ibid. : 60-82; 364-371).

Meanwhile there were about 1,500 people, mostly dependents of the KMT troops, who arrived in northern Thailand. They were tacitly allowed to stay by the Thai government. The first three KMT refugee villages were founded in 1954.

After the first evacuation, there were still about 5,000-7,000 KMT troops remaining in Burma (ibid. : 27). Though the Taiwanese government stated officially that it would not have any responsibility for those who had not been evacuated to Taiwan, the link between the remnant troops and Taiwan was not really severed. After international attention became quiescent, the Taiwanese government decided to recover its forces in Burma. General Liu Uan-Lieu was sent to reorganize the remnant troops in November 1954. Supplies and training programs from Taiwan were sent again. The new force was named "Yunnanese Anti-Communist Voluntary Army" (ibid. : 27; T'an 1984: 482-483). Its headquarters was established in Lai Lang[3].

More soldiers were recruited. In early 1956, there were about 6,000; by the end of 1958, there were about 9,000; and in June 1960, the number increased to 9,718 (Ministry of Information, Taiwan 1964: 91,97,229). The Burmese government was aware of the KMT development. Fighting between the two continued to occur. The Burmese government finally cooperated with the Chinese Communists and defeated these obstinate KMT troops.

A second evacuation then took place. There were only 4,406 people evacuated in 1961 (ibid. : 100-110). But many soldiers and dependents decided not to be evacuated. Though the Nationalist government was in Taiwan now, the island was strange for them; instead northern Thailand was closer to their homeland, where many of them still hoped to return someday. Among the remnants, there were two major troops which still sustained their military formation. One was the Third Army led by Lee Wen-Huan; the other was the Fifth Army led by Duan Hsi-Wen. They numbered around 3,000.

Lee and Duan decided to develop their future in northern Thailand with self sufficiency achieved through drug trafficking and trading in jade, gems and other goods. They knew they did not belong to any powerful military factions in Taiwan. Their future was unpredictable there. In the frontier area of northern Thailand, they could build up their sphere of influence again. They might be nobodies in Taiwan but rulers with some power in northern Thailand, a still rather unlawful area. They brought some troops to northern Thailand and entrenched themselves along the Thai-Burmese border. Many dependents and other civilian refugees gradually followed and resettled in various villages.

## 1.2 *Decision-Making and Power Reservation in Involuntary Migration*

Like other cases of refugee flight, the fleeing of the KMT Yunnanese Chinese and other civilian refugees belongs to forced migration or involuntary migration. This type of migration often results in uprooting, deprivation and dislocation. It is a fundamental break from one's familiar environment, social relationships, cultural norms, values, etc. During the flight, a refugee confronts a series of traumatic experiences, which bring him/ her into a state of distrust (Daniel and Knudsen, eds. 1995).

Kunz (1973) applies the push-pull theory to distinguish voluntary migration from involuntary migration. The former is basically motivated by the pull factor of the immigrant country, which is perceived as offering greater opportunities to improve the immigrant's life. The latter is caused primarily by the push factor of the refugee's native country, which is perceived as threatening his/her life. Kunz's theory is widely referred to. However he and many other social scientists overemphasize the push factor in involuntary migration, and regard refugees merely as passive and powerless. He calls the refugee's movement "kinetic", which "resembles the movement of the billiard ball: devoid of inner direction...." (Kunz 1973: 131)

In the book edited by Hansen and Oliver-Smith (1982), Kunz's theory was challenged by the case studies presented inside. Also the present case of the KMT, with their complex military background, deviates from Kunz's kinetic theory. Though refugees flee from their homeland primarily because of the "overwhelming" push factor (Kunz 1973: 132), they are not merely passive or powerless. The obstinate KMT and other civilian refugees are actors responsible for their decision to flee (Mangalam 1968; Hansen and Oliver-Smith 1982). Their perception of and response to the situation they were confronting reveal their inner directions of protecting themselves from outer threats and persecutions impending over them, and of preserving whatever power they could exert and control.

The KMT remnants, belonging to different military units in Yunnan, quickly united together, after arriving in Burma. They tried to restore communication with Taiwan and seek help from local earlier Chinese immigrants. Despite the fact that they were poorly equipped at the beginning, staying together helped to generate a sort of power, and the common ideal of fighting back to homeland re-enforced group coherence. The linkage with Taiwan was recovered quickly, which galvanized the troops' morale. They believed that the government they served was also working on the same goal in Taiwan as they were in Burma. Though guerrilla life in an unwelcoming country was harsh, they sustained themselves with the "noble mission" of liberation of their compatriots from the communist regime and were spurred on by the praise of their highest leader in his telegram of 1951, that their revolutionary spirit was glorious. In their minds, they were fighting for justice. The Chinese Communists were evil and would be finally punished. Their belief created a sort of power too.

They looked for whatever help they could gain. There was support from Taiwan, earlier Chinese immigrants and the US. These were their material sources. Cooperation with local ethnic rebels was another means. Nevertheless, among the troops, there were also factions and struggle. Some unit leaders exploited their military means to gain personal wealth and power. The officers sent from Taiwan suffered from lack of credibility among the different troops, especially after the first evacuation. During the evacuations, there were agreements and disagreements. Some advocated that the area they stayed was originally Chinese territory and that they had the right to rule over the people (Hu 1977). These phenomena illuminated the KMT's internal diversities which would not have existed if they had been merely passive and powerless.

For the civilian refugees, their flight also demonstrated their inner directions. Before the Chinese Communists arrived in Yunnan, some people had already fled. They are called anticipatory refugees by Kunz (Kunz 1973: 131-132). Most of them belonged to the landlord class which was the first target for class struggle by the Communists. Though they could not take their land with them, many took their papers of landholdings, valuable articles, and laborers and tenants who joined them. After the Chinese Communists gained control of Yunnan and class struggle took place, more people belonging to the landowning class escaped. Many other civilian refugees also fled their homeland individually or in groups throughout the 1950s and 1960s as different political movements were undertaken, which caused serious famines and persecutions. The people of these later groups were called acute refugees by Kunz (ibid. : 132-133).

Although flight is mostly carried out in haste, it results from a series of decision-making based on all possible alternatives, and not simply blind action. Some Yunnanese decided to flee earlier, others later. To use Kunz's terminology, there were different "vintages" (ibid. : 140). They had to decide when to flee, who would leave and who had to be left behind, what to bring with them, which way they would flee, if they would flee in groups or individually, where and to whom they would go to after arriving in the neighboring country, etc.

Many civilian refugees joined the KMT guerrillas. The earlier refugees were mostly males. People thought that the Communists would not do too much harm to women, children and old people. Families sent young males out first. Some joined the local self-defense guards to fight against the local communists and fled with the guards later. These guards became small units of the KMT guerrillas in Burma. Their membership was based on kinship and places of origin. The Third Army, led by Lee Wen-Huan, was originally such a unit. Civilian refugees and dependents of the troops were more or less following the troops' movement in order to gain protection.

In sum, involuntary migration should not be regarded as kinetic movement; nor is flight simply "a physical expression of the refugee's feeling of being helpless and powerless" (Kibreab 1987: 37). Refugees have their particular backgrounds, cultural heritage, goals, etc. which are influencing factors in their flight and later resettlement. Although they suffer "multifaceted loss" (Hansen 1982: 14), most of them would like to do their best to recover from the loss with whatever means they find. In the following section, the KMT resettlement in northern Thailand will further substantiate this truth.

## 2. Resettlement in Northern Thailand

### 2.1 *The Story of the Third and the Fifth Armies*

The decision to enter northern Thailand meant a departure from the earlier mission period. Fighting back to Yunnan would be rather impossible with the small number of troops the Third and the Fifth Armies had. Both Lee and Duan were aware that their new goal was to survive in northern Thailand. The entry of the ex-KMT military forces and civilian refugees was tacitly accepted by the Thai government. The troops were stationed in a few places along the Thai-Burmese border. The Thai government thought that these anti-communist corps could help to bolster the security of northern Thailand. Thailand and Burma had a long history of enmity with each other. Moreover, civil wars were going on in

Indochina. Thailand wanted to stop the communist infiltration into its country. Yet, for the concern of national sovereignty, the Thai government required these ex-KMT troops, on their arrival, not to undertake military activities inside the country.

In order to finance their troops, Lee and Duan engaged in drug trafficking in the 1960s. After the second evacuation, Taiwan no longer gave any supplies to the remnant troops. Many soldiers of the Third and the Fifth Armies were still stationed in Shan states to protect "goods" from being robbed by the Burmese army or other rebel groups. Businessmen entrusted Lee or Duan to buy opium or heroin for them, and after the "goods" were escorted to Thailand, they would pay tax as protection fees to Lee or Duan. In 1969, Duan and Lee accepted the Thai government's request (under the pressure of the US) to stop trading in narcotics anymore. They sold all the narcotics they had to the government (compensated for the loss by the US). Afterwards Lee and Duan only traded in gems and jade, but some of their subordinates still engaged in this contraband trade secretly.

For the first ten years in Thailand, the status of the ex-KMT troops and other civilian refugees was not officially accepted. Discussions were held between the Taiwanese government, the Thai government and Lee and Duan, but no result was obtained until 1970. The Taiwanese government then assured the Thai government it would not evacuate these troops to Taiwan, and also Lee and Duan refused to go to Taiwan. Only then were the latter openly accepted by the Thai government with a request to cooperate with the Thai military to suppress the communist forces in Thailand. Lee and Duan understood that it was a means for them to gain legal status and also an opportunity to demonstrate their loyalty to the Thai government. They accepted the request and were guaranteed supplies to maintain a part of their troops[4]. They accomplished a few missions. Two important ones were the battles at Mt. Phamong and Mt. Phayao in the early 1970s, and the ones at Mt. Khawya in 1981. The battles of 1981 were rather difficult because most of the soldiers were not young anymore, and military training was not given continuously during normal times. Mr. Chen, the former general director of the mission recalled that before the campaign, he told the soldiers: "We can only win and not lose the battle. The Thai government asks us to help to fight because they think we are good.... If we lose, we will not be able to stay in Thailand afterwards." A number of their brothers died or were injured in the campaigns. Their contribution was recognized by the Thai government, different levels of legal status were granted gradually to the troops, their dependents and other civilian refugees. Retired ex-KMT soldiers often emphasize that their Thai citizenship has been granted at the expense of their blood.

The Thai Communists gradually died out in the 1980s. The aging ex-KMT troops were finally disbanded in 1987-1989, but disintegration of the troops already started since the early 1980s. Duan Shi-Wen died in 1980. He was replaced by Lei Yu-Tien, but Lei's leadership was not able to unite the whole Fifth Army. There was a power struggle within the troop. With regard to the Third Army, Lee Wen-Huan has gradually entrusted his work to his son and two daughters since the early 1980s. He is now an ailing patriarch. The junior Lees still exert some minimal influence among a few refugee villages, but informants said that once their father passed away, the influence of the Lee family would diminish. Villagers often expressed their contempt toward the second generation of Lees.

## 2.2 *The Story of the KMT Refugee Villages*

Most dependents and other civilian refugees arrived in northern Thailand in the 1960s and the 1970s. They were mainly escorted by the troops from Burma to Thailand. Most of the early Yunnanese refugee villages developed around the military bases of the troops. They were located in isolated border areas. Generally speaking, the Third Army had influence over the villages of Chiang Mai province, and the Fifth Army over those of Chiang Rai province. According to the 1974 census conducted by the Thai government in 12 major KMT villages, there were 11,100 Yunnanese refugees (Prakatwuttisan 1995: 198-199)[5].

These villages had been rather isolated from Thai society. Before gaining their legal status, the Yunnanese refugees were confined within their villages. If they wanted to leave for another district, they had to get a pass permit from the local immigration office first. Communication between them and Thai people was very limited. There was a feeling of distrust toward each other. Thai people were afraid of these armed Yunnanese troops. They have been calling the latter "ciin ho". The origination of the term is not sure anymore, but it is used with a pejorative meaning toward the Yunnanese Chinese for being backward, violent and dealing in drug trafficking. In contrast, the Yunnanese people were afraid of local Thais too, whom they have been referring to as "kuolo". Its origination is not known either, but the Yunnanese refer to "kuolo" as barbarous. Informants stress that they had to carry weapons or were in groups when they left the villages in the earlier period, otherwise they ran the risk of being robbed or killed by "kuolo".

Life during the early resettlement period was harsh. People had to open up wild land and built their thatched houses with their own hands. The only means of transportation was on horseback or by foot. During the rainy season, the road became so muddy that it was very difficult to pass. Whenever there was an emergency, conditions seemed to be unbearable. Most men were in the troops or away for organized trade to Burma. Women had to run the house all alone, including making a living for the family, because the troops only supplied rationed rice. They grew rice, maize, vegetables, beans, taro, etc. They also raised chickens and pigs, and brewed rice wine. Some women were also hired by Thai farmers for a few bath a day. Though life was not easy, it gradually became stable.

In every village, there is a self-governing committee organized by villagers themselves, taking care of the village's affairs, such as construction of the infrastructure system, Chinese education, some major ritual and festival ceremonies, the village's security, dispute settlement and sometimes also family matters like divorce. In the earlier days, most village heads were appointed by the troops. Nowadays, they are mostly elected by villagers; except in a few villages in which the Lee family still exerts some influence.

The inflows of Yunnanese refugees have been continuous due to political instability in China and in Burma. According to data of 1994 released by the Free China Relief Association in northern Thailand (see following), there were more than 60,000 Yunnanese refugees in 77 villages. Apart from the KMT villages established by the armies, many new ones were established by retired soldiers, which gradually attracted more new arrivals from Burma. Many new arrivals were relatives of the earlier ones. Many of them do not have legal status in Thailand. Their movement is very mobile. They often only stay in villages for a while, and then go to Bangkok for work.

The living conditions of most villages have improved a great deal nowadays. The Free China Relief Association, which is a semi-official organization in Taiwan, has had a work group in northern Thailand since 1982. It has greatly helped KMT refugee villages with their infrastructure system, Chinese education, medical care, agriculture, etc. It also gave full grants to students for further studies in Taiwan before 1992.

Most of the refugee villages have electricity connections. Many families have televisions. Some villagers set up satellite receivers and connected lines to other houses. People can thus watch Chinese programs from Taiwan, Hong Kong and China.

Beside television, the newspaper is another source to learn about the outside world. The Universal Daily Newspaper, which is in Chinese, is available in many villages. It is run by a large Taiwanese newspaper enterprise. The subscription fee is about half of the regular price in these villages.

Most villages are like a well functioning body, with a market place, Thai and Chinese primary schools and a Kuan-yin (a popular goddess among Yunnanese) temple. Some big villages also have a post office and a clinic. General merchandise shops are widespread. People can purchase almost everything they need in the villages. After a few decades of resettlement, these KMT refugee villages are still very much on their own. Communication with Thai society is limited.

## 2.3 *The Socio-Cultural Resettlement*

Although not every village location is self-chosen, KMT refugee villages resemble the "self-settled villages" in Hansen's case study on Angolan refugees in Zambia (Hansen 1982). The Yunnanese refugees have their autonomy within their villages. They have their own socio-political structure sustained by a power hierarchy which was closely connected with the troops in the past. To understand the resettlement of KMT Yunnanese Chinese refugees, both the troops and the villages must be studied.

With regard to the troops, they provided protection to the villages and served as an ethnic emblem for group cohesion. It was the troops which brought most of Yunnanese refugees to northern Thailand in the 1960s and the 1970s. They established many refugee villages for their dependents, other civilian followers and the refugees who arrived later. New arrivals had to get residential permission from village heads or the troops in order to settle down. They often established their socio-political links with the troops or some key persons in the villages through their relatives (no matter real or affiliated) who had already lived in these villages. The existence of the troops guaranteed the villages' security. Moreover, the victories in the battles they fought for the Thai government helped Yunnanese refugees to gain legal status. Informants often say that without the troops, they would have all become "kuolo".

The existence of the villages, on the other hand, has helped the Yunnanese to recover from the multifaceted loss in flight. They have been providing the primary function of stability and security. Women could retreat to their familiar customs and organize life in the Yunnanese way. They have been cooking Yunnanese food, celebrating Yunnanese Chinese festivals, observing their traditional values, worshipping their ancestors and other Chinese gods, etc. The way of "clinging to the familiar and changing no more than is necessary" in a strange environment is termed "conservative strategy" (Scudder and Colson 1982: 272). Many studies on refugees' resettlement also present a similar pattern (Shami 1993; Hansen and Oliver-Smith, eds. 1982; Daniel and Knudsen, eds. 1995; Gold 1992). Through the conservative strategy, refugees continue to uphold their own traditions and transfer them to the next generation. How successfully the culture can be preserved and continued varies from case to case.

What is interesting with the present KMT case is that women have played the primary role concerning the continuity of Yunnanese tradition, for men were away for their military duties in the earlier days.

Life within the refugee villages has linked the Yunnanese people's past with their present and given hopes toward the future. Women have not only organized their family life in a Yunnanese way, they have applied their familiar skills to make a living. They used to make clothes, shoes, pickled food and brewed rice wine for sale. This was the work they were familiar with in Yunnan. In this case, women have been the first safeguard of tradition. They have done their best to improve living conditions and raise the second generation in whom they see future and hope. Knudsen explains the linkage of past, present and future in his thesis on Vietnamese refugees in Denmark:

> ...if the refugees were to survive as social persons, they had to establish some continuity, trying together past, present and future. This was not only true of their attempts to reestablish meaning in their life courses, it was also a key feature of daily exile life, expressed when refugees talked about dilemmas concerning the present and the future. (Knudsen 1988: 12)

The linkage entails the recovery of meaning and cultural continuity which also helps to reconstruct the refugee's self-identity and the basis of trust (Daniel and Knudsen 1995: 4). Within the villages, life is familiar; things are Yunnanese. Villagers know each other. Many are relatives (in flexible terms) or people from the same native region. Moreover, they have shared the same experiences of flight from Yunnan to Burma and then to northern Thailand. Each village is a small Yunnanese society. The outside of the village is associated with strangeness, danger and mistrust. In sum, the refugee villages have been a kind of bulwark which offered physical and psychological niches for their security, cultural continuity, recovery of self-identity and a basis of trust.

The existence of Yunnanese communities in northern Thailand is attributed to both the troop and the refugee villages. The former were composed of men and the later primarily of women. Both were complementary to each other in the past[6]. However the complementarity suffered a rupture when the troops were dissolved in 1987-1989, and also with the continual departure of the second generation from the villages to Taiwan for further studies or work, or to Thai cities for ever.

It has been mentioned above that the troops had the function of cohesion among the Yunnanese refugees. The function was maintained with hierarchical control. Lee and Duan were their highest leaders. Together with other officials of the troops and village heads, they formed the top echelon of the hierarchy and were referred to as "the top people". By contrast, common villagers remained as "the low people". The foreign and difficult environment pushed Yunnanese refugees to stick together. Most of the new arrivals joined the earlier ones in the established villages to ensure their security and to obtain legal status through their relatives of the villages or the troops. Orders from "the top people" were to be followed. Those who deviated from the rules were punished. However, as pointed out earlier, disintegration of the troops took place in the early 1980s. There were power struggles, especially in the Fifth Army. In addition, most solders were getting old, and the younger generation did not see their future in the troops. The spirit of the armies was weakening. Apart from these internal changes, external factors accelerated the disbandment of the armies. Thai communist forces were dying out in the 1980s, and the Thai government did not like to see the continual existence of the KMT foreign armies. The supplies from the Thai government were reduced annually since 1984, and were totally stopped in 1987. The Fifth Army was disbanded then, and the Third Army in 1989. Fragmentation stalks the KMT Yunnanese communities, following the disintegration of the troops and their final disbandment. The discourse of power hierarchy is disappearing in the villages. Each village has become more civil and independent.

The continuous migration of the second generation from the villages to Taiwan or cities of Thailand is another factor affecting the former continuity in meaning and culture. The villages have functioned as the niches for the linkage of the first generation's past, present and future. Their future is anchored in the second generation, but the second generation do not see their future in these villages.

After obtaining Thai citizenship, they prefer to discard their refugee status and the stigma of being "ciin ho". Taiwan has been the first desired place for further migration in the last 20 years, partly due to its successful economic development and partly due to the emotional link with "their fatherland". From the Chinese education, which is sponsored by Taiwan and given in the villages, the youngsters have been taught that their fatherland is the Republic of China in Taiwan. For many of the second generation, it has been a great dream to go there for further studies. After studies, many have got married and settled in Taiwan. In the last 10 to 15 years, a great number of Yunnanese youngsters have also been to Taiwan as foreign laborers. Some have managed to stay after the contract period. Those who returned to Thailand, mostly continue to work in cities. Being a farmer in the refugee village is not attractive to them.

What we have seen from the first and second generations of the KMT Yunnanese Chinese of northern Thailand is that the involuntary migration of the former changes to voluntary migration of the latter. Will the Yunnanese communities disappear following the breakup of the Yunnanese villages? This question will be examined in more detail in the following section concerning the ethnic identification of the people.

## 3. The ethnic identification of the KMT Yunnanese Chinese

When one enters a Yunnanese village in northern Thailand, one will immediately recognize its Yunnanese Chinese character by the language people speak, housing arrangements, Chinese temples, the Chinese school, the Chinese cemetery, etc. But one will also gradually notice that most villagers are the first generation immigrants and the latecomers often only stay in the village for a short while and then leave for work in Thai cities.

What does this reveal about the people's ethnic identification? The author uses the term ethnic identification instead of ethnic identity, because the former indicates the process of identifying which bears both subjective and objective dimensions and the latter is essentially a subjective matter. The author agrees with Epstein that although the fundamental basis in identity is a matter of perception from the subjective/ internal aspect, it is influenced by the social environment, namely the objective/ situational aspect (Epstein 1978: 27). Members of an ethnic group balance themselves between these two aspects by "situational selection" in order to avoid conflicts or schizoid tendencies (ibid. : 26). Therefore ethnic identification is a process of interaction between subjective perception and objective circumstances. Subjective perception derives from a feeling of belonging and continuity and the emblematic use of any aspect of culture (De Vos 1975: 17). Objective circumstances include any external factor from the environment the member stays in or relates to. Ethnic identity is fluid under different historical contexts. Its salience ebbs and flows over time. Hutnik says: "individuals continually strive to place and define themselves in the world of relationships and meanings.... Thus ethnic identity is arrived at by a process of what Chun (1983) calls 'socioepistemic self-emplacement'." (Hutnik 1991: 20)

For the first generation, their feeling of belonging and continuity links with their very particular and traumatic experiences of flight. Life in the past was replete with experiences of fighting and fleeing. Many men fought against the Japanese, then the Chinese Communists in China, and the Burmese army in Burma and then the Thai Communists in Thailand. The ex-KMT remnants in northern Thailand have survived from one battle to another, and from one retreat to another. Their memories were haunted with fear, blood, death, hunger, diseases, etc. For the women, though not participating in fighting directly, their experiences were no less bitter. While fleeing, they had to take care of their children or other family members, like parents or parents-in-law. Several informants related the story that some of the women had been too weak to carry their small children or babies while fleeing, and that they had to leave them on the way and hoped that some kind people would carry them and raise them. There were also women who gave birth while fleeing. Women had to look for food or make a living for the family while in Burma and then in northern Thailand. Many of their husbands were in the troops and returned home only very occasionally.

Women of the first generation lived under great stress caused by poverty, worries for their husbands' safety, children's illnesses, fear of each new environment they arrived in, etc.

Both men and women of the first generation have undergone many traumatic experiences. Nevertheless, under the harsh living conditions, a feeling of belonging and continuity has been strengthened. Many see themselves as victims of history and link their traumatic experiences with the long Chinese history which is seen as a history replete with disasters, social and political upheavals. They often say that Chinese people are plagued by frequent ills (tuo tsai tuo nan). According to De Vos's psychocultural approach, a feeling of continuity relates an individual to his or her group with a collective memory of the past and a perspective into the future. It is a "sense of personal survival in the historical continuity of the group" (De Vos 1975: 17). For the KMT Chinese, it is this sense of survival which enabled them to confront various hardships in the past and also galvanized their feeling of belonging and continuity for their Yunnanese Chinese ethnic identity. They perceive themselves as a particular group of Chinese living in northern Thailand, who are distinguished from a great number of earlier Chinese immigrants in Thailand.

On the emblematic aspect, the conservative strategy has been applied as mentioned above. Adopting a Yunnanese lifestyle has been an important means to continue life on this foreign soil. The existence of refugee villages, functioning as self-settled villages, allows this strategy to be carried out. It has linked up the people's past with their present and offered hopes of their future in the second generation.

With respect to the objective circumstances, the direct contact between the first generation and Thai society has been very limited. Nevertheless, contacts between them do exist, though they mostly may be seen as indirect. The term "ethnic group" is meaningful only when it suggests "contacts and interrelationship" (Eriksen 1993: 9) with others, whether direct or indirect. The KMT Yunnanese Chinese are aware of being in Thai society, where there are "kuolo" and hill tribe people. The relationships with the former are based on distrust. They regard themselves as more superior in culture and morality than both "kuolo" and hill tribe people. However, they are also aware of the importance of obtaining legal status. They fought for the Thai government to demonstrate their loyalty to Thailand. Informants state that they are Thai citizens for the means of survival, but they are Chinese forever in their blood.

The first generation has also tried to transmit this subjective feeling of belonging and continuity to the second generation, not just in the way of daily living, but also through Chinese education. Students go to the Thai school during the day and to the Chinese school in the evening. Chinese education was given secretly even during the period when it was banned by the Thai government in the second half of the 1980s. It seems that the Yunnanese Chinese ethnic identity will continue to persist in the second generation, but the author discovered that the reality is more complex than it appears to be.

It is true that being brought up in these refugee villages, many of the second generation have a sharp memory of their fathers' frequent absence during their childhood and the poverty which they and their mothers had gone through. For the families which have lived in the villages where the troops were stationed, the children grew up with a vivid memory of the troops. They saw them wearing uniforms and  engaging in training exercises and were used to the arrival and departure of the trade caravans. Since childhood, they have been aware of being refugees. Nevertheless they have also absorbed the Thai way to a certain degree through Thai education, television programs and contacts with Thai society, especially after they have moved to urban areas. There exists a kind of complex in their subjective perception of self-identity. It has been said that meaning flourishes when the past is linked with the present and some hopes are foreseen in the future. The problem with the second generation is the past, which does not simply mean one's childhood, but an extension with and understanding of one's group's collective memory in history and culture. Many informants of the second generation express their identity complex by saying that they are regarded as "ciin ho" in Thailand and overseas Chinese in Taiwan. They are not complete in either society. They sometimes find themselves handicapped in the use of languages. They are not able to express themselves thoroughly in either Chinese or Thai. They do not feel they have a tradition to fall back on like their parents do. They know Yunnanese customs only superficially and in piecemeal. Besides, they have a sense of inferiority and are not willing to be recognized as "ciin ho" in Thai society or Yunnanese Chinese refugees of northern Thailand in Taiwan. Many also express their contempt for hierarchical control of the villages in the past. On the one hand, they have a strong feeling of identification with the villages, but on the other, many do not feel free or confident to express this feeling and identity[7].

Those who have settled in Thai cities, mostly in Chiang Rai, Chiang Mai and Bangkok, adapt to the Thai way, at least in the public domain. If they can afford to, they send their children to private Thai schools, which are considered better. Some still speak Yunnanese with their children at home or send them to learn some Chinese in the weekends.

The third generation is likely to be more Thai in their way of living and behavior, but this does not presume a total transformation in ethnic identity. The collective memory in history and culture and emblematic use of culture can be recreated when objective circumstances inspire (Roosens 1989). There has been a trend of reassertion of Chinese ethnicity since the last decade among the offspring of earlier Chinese immigrants in Thailand. It is widely recognized that Thai society has absorbed a lot of Chinese elements in spite of the government's preference for an assimilation policy.

After the disbandment of the troops, the Yunnanese communities have become more segmented, but solidarity at the subgroup level still exists and functions. New networks based on kinship and religion (mostly of Christian and Muslim churches) are developed and serve as a kind of bridge between the villages and the cities. The continuous arrivals of Yunnanese from Burma has helped to maintained Yunnanese tradition in the refugees villages, despite the highly mobile nature of these groups of immigrants. However, questions regarding the perpetuation of Yunnanese Chinese communities and survival of their ethnic identity in the future demand further study.

*Notes*

1. The KMT stands for the Kuomintang (or the Nationalist party) led by Chiang Kai-Shek then. After losing mainland China, Chiang withdrew to Taiwan with his followers. The KMT has been the majority political party since then.

2. It is unclear who defeated whom in this and many later campaigns between the KMT and the Brumese army. According to the latter, the KMT were defeated, but information provided by ex-KMT remnants and Taiwanese government point to KMT victory. While narrating their past history in Burma, informants often emphasize how undisciplined the Burmese troops were and how courageously they fought against the Burmese each time, though their troop number was far less than the Burmese.

3. In 1957, it was moved to Keng Lap.

4. The regular troops of the Third and the Fifth Armies increased to around 5,000-6,000. The Thai government gave supplies to 1,500 ex-KMT soldiers (750 for each army).

5. Yet the census was not thorough. Based on the author's field research and other relevant data, there had been about 29 KMT Yunnanese villages (Chang 1999: 101).

6. This complementarity of "female" villages and "male" troops may best be explained through the Chinese yin-yang rationale. Yin, representing the female, and yang, representing the male, are structuring components of social life in Chinese self-perception (Chang 1999).

7. For a more detailed study on the generation classification of the KMT Yunnanese Chinese with reference to their ethnic identification, see Chang (1999) chapters 7 and 12, or Chang (2000).

# Chapter IV:

## Ethnicity, Language and Religion of the Suryoye

**Kathleen Ghequière**

*Syrians, Assyrians, Chaldeans, Aramaeans,*
*If we unite,*
*What will happen then?* (Tuma Nahroyo)

### 1. The name of the group and the myths of common descent

The community that we will discuss in this chapter is a Christian community consisting mainly of Syrian Orthodox believers and Chaldeans. Though the community originates in Southeast Turkey, many of its members now live in the Belgian capital Brussels, where our research was in fact conducted (1990-1996).

Of all the territories that ever belonged to the Ottoman Empire, present-day Turkey is the region where, until the end of the 19th century, Christianity was most prevalent. In Istanbul, there was an Armenian and a Greek Orthodox community living in relative comfort. And in Turkish Kurdistan, from Lake Van to the Tur`Abdin ('the mountain range of God's servants'), the Jacobites and the Assyrians used to live alongside the local Muslim population. In the course of history, there have been numerous periods in which the Christians were persecuted, but the 19th century was an era of relatively peaceful coexistence. Nowadays, however, Turkey has the smallest proportion of Christians in the entire Middle East. And in Turkish Kurdistan they have, in fact, all but disappeared.

There are two contributing factors to the build-up of their ethnicity in migration at the end of the 20th century. A first element is the age-old division of the Churches, which has created a situation that to most Occidentals seems an inextricable tangle. Secondly, there is the external process of expulsion of Christians which actually started at the beginning of this century and accelerated in the 1970s and 1980s. In this chapter, we shall focus on the shifts that have taken place in the ethnic discourse of the members of this community as a result of a re-interpretation of their ethnic identity.

It was clear from the beginning that writing or speaking about this community would not be an easy matter. For one thing, it is not self-evident how this group of people should be referred to, as their name has been the subject of a long-lasting internal dispute. The mere discussion about what is the proper name of the community implies certain positions with regard to ethnicity. The term 'Assyrian-Chaldean', for instance, was used by the French mandate in Syria to refer to the soldiers serving in the special forces of the Levant. This name enabled the French to ignore the distinction between different religious communities. The same is happening today in migration: Religious differences, which used to be so important and still are to many people, are transcended -especially by the younger generation- when referring to the entire community of Mesopotamian Christians.

But as the name of the community is the subject of many discussions, it is by no means easy to find a general term for these people that is acceptable to the entire research population. The name Christian-Turkish, for instance, is met with disdain within the community itself, because it is felt to define their nationality as 'Turkish'. The term *Suryoye* (the Syrian term for -Syrian- Christians) appears to be least problematic in the eyes of most members of the community. We shall therefore use this term systematically throughout this article when referring to the entire group, while we shall use the term *Suryoyo* to refer to individuals[1]. Any other term refers directly to the internal discussion regarding the interpretation of the ethnic identity.

From the moment one writes or speaks about the *Suryoye* one adopts a position in their ethnic debate. Even the question of where their history starts is charged with emotion. Their myth of origin, or their myth of common descent, is essential to their ethnic identity. And precisely this myth is subject of dispute.

"But we are all related: If we were to draw up a genealogy of all families and go back in time as far as we could, we would find that all of us are descended from Abraham" (interview with S., 54 yrs.).
Kulan ahilna (We are all related).

The strong kinship with Abraham is a recurring theme. The following passage in Genesis is often quoted in this respect: "*God said to Abraham, 'Look up into heaven and count the stars if you can. Such will your descendants be*'" (Gen 15,5).

The story of Abraham's 'migration' is central to many lines of reasoning and legitimizations. They regard themselves as the direct descendants of Abraham and, following Abraham's example, they had to leave their native region, to which they might never return but will continue to refer, and travelled to the Promised Land which henceforth is the affluent Christian Occident.

The notion of their direct lineage from Abraham is central to the entire community. But although Abraham is, in this respect, a unifying factor, he fulfils this function from different ethnic angles. On the one hand, reference is made to the father of Abraham, who hails from Ur in the Assyrian empire. On the other, reference is made to Abraham and his descendants, who lived in Haran in the Southeast of Turkey.

This different ethnic positioning is directly connected with another reference to a common lineage. The starting point of many studies of the *Suryoye* in Turkey lies in the early years of Christianity (Valognes 1994; Anschütz 1985; et al...). There are good grounds for this, as the group in question explicitly presents itself as being Christian. Moreover, it was during the first centuries of Christianity that the antagonism arose within the community in Southeast Turkey which continues to divide them today in Brussels and elsewhere in Europe where they have found shelter as political refugees.

According to most *Suryoye*, their history goes back to the Aramaic tribes, amongst whom Abraham once lived as the archetypical father, and where Christian evangelisation actually began to take shape. The evangelisation happened in Aramaic, which is still the language of many Christians in Turkey, and this process resulted in a Church; the 'original Church', the cradle of Christendom[2].

Other *Suryoye* situate their origins in the heyday of the Assyrian Empire. Adherents of this theory too underline the historical significance of their community to the Occident, not so much from a religious perspective, but from a technical, judicial and scientific point of view.

This division roughly corresponds to that between the Syrian Orthodox Church and the Assyrian or Nestorian Church, but it is increasingly interpreted ethnically. 'Aramaean' is opposed to 'Assyrian'. The name *Suryoye* is sometimes used as a common name for the entire group, but this is not acceptable to everyone, as it is also quite often used as a synonym for 'Aramaeans'.

In the eyes of some, the term *Suryoye* refers to the Syrian Orthodox Church, thus underlining the 'metaphorical affinity' of the Aramaic tribes that have converted to Christianity. This point of view concurs with the official position of the Syrian Orthodox Church, which distances itself in this matter from the East Syrian Church. As the word 'Aramaean' is used quite often in the Old Testament, a link is easily established between the term *Suryoye* and the evangelization of the Aramaic tribes.

According to the patriarch, the political and cultural movements in the diaspora should not waste their energy on disputes about the name of the community. On 14 August 1994, during the consecration of the Church of the Virgin Mary at a monastery in Glane (The Netherlands), the patriarch Mor Igniatius Zakka I Iwas[3] said the following: 'We should all stand under the umbrella of the church. The name of the church, the people and the language is and will always be *Suryoyo*'. He added that the church is not opposed to progressive ideas (*rinje imsonoye*) insofar as they remain outside the church.

Secondly, the term *Suryoye* can be seen as a common term that is acceptable to Aramaeans, Assyrians and Chaldeans. According to this view, the specific names of these communities are merely a reflection of a secondary division, based on their specific sub-ethnic history, e.g. that of the Aramaic tribes, the Assyrian Empire and The Chaldean Empire.

In a third interpretation, the term *Suryoye* is equated with the Assyrians. The word *Suryoyo* is, according to this view, derived from the word *(a)suryoyo*. It is argued that the vowel *a* is simply not always pronounced. As this is also the case with numerous other words, many regard this to be a plausible theory.

Generally speaking, there are two opposing groups: Those who consider themselves as descendants of the Aramaeans, and those who look upon themselves as direct descendants of the Assyrians. Both groups are constantly looking for 'scientific' arguments to substantiate their theory.

The 'Assyrians' reject religion as the criterion for membership of the community. They argue that the Syrian Orthodox group, the Syrian Catholics, the Syrian Protestants, the Chaldeans and Nestorians all belong to a single community through their common Assyrian past. To them the secular character of the Church is of central importance. Here are three examples of 'scientific' arguments supporting the 'Assyrian' view:

"We are not Aramaeans. Those who claim that we are don't even know what the term actually means. It means nothing more than 'the highlands'. When they say that Jesus spoke Aramaic, all this means is that he spoke the language of the people of the highlands. And 'the people of Canaan' actually means the people of the lowlands" (G.Y., 35 yrs.).

"The Assyrian Empire is the basis of Occidental culture. We are Occidental; we are the actual foundation of this culture" (idem).

"Our people has existed for 2500 years and, in the course of history, we have been overrun by the Persians, the Medes, the Byzantines, the Arabs, the Turks and the Kurds. So why should we disappear now? We may be threatened as a group, but if, after all those centuries, we still speak the same language, then what is there to be afraid of?" (S.E., 64 y.).

There are families in which some members call themselves Aramaean while others call themselves Assyrian. The ones will refer to the Church and Christianity as the basis of unity within group, and believe that this is the best way to position themselves in the Occident; the others will refer to the foundations of Occidental culture, transcending the religious debate.

The question of what is the correct name of the community, coupled with the question of ancestry and its implications for the religious interpretation of ethnicity, is charged with emotion. After all, the term 'Assyrian' has, in the course of history, come to be associated with the search for an independent homeland, and has thus assumed a political undertone. So clearly the repositioning of a group by means of its name has all kinds of historical and emotional connotations.

The history of the Syrian Orthodox community cannot be compared to that of the Armenians or the Nestorians (referred to as Assyrians by the British) and their struggle for independence in Southeast Turkey. The Syrian Orthodox community has always remained loyal to the Turks. They have never tried to acquire independence, nor are they nationalistic. The persecution of Syrian Orthodox believers can only be explained from a religious and socio-economic perspective, as a result of their relative well-being.

The Syrian Orthodox community merely wants to orient itself religiously and does not wish to occupy itself with other matters.

As mentioned above, the process of *Suryoye*-migration accelerated in the 1970s. In 1975, for instance, Sweden was faced with a flood of *Suryoye* refugees. Some were protestant, others Catholic and a minority were Nestorian. When the Swedish authorities labelled them all as Assyrians (which traditionally applies to the Nestorians only) this caused a conflict within the *Suryoye* community.

The conflict did not merely concern the confusion of the Nestorians with the Syrian Orthodox group. It mainly revolved around the politico-nationalist position that is connected with the name 'Assyrian'. It was not merely about two distinct Churches (the West Syrian and the East Syrian Church, each with its own schisms), but also concerned a political issue within the *Suryoye* community.

Although the majority of *Suryoye* belong to the Syrian Orthodox church, the Assyrian nationalist movement has become increasingly influential within this group. It is the politico-nationalist perspective which causes difficulties within their Churches. While in its original meaning the term 'Assyrians' referred exclusively to the Nestorians, it now has a political connotation, from which the Syrian Orthodox church has distanced itself. The 'Assyrians' in Western Europe are not at all in favour of a political independence movement, but they are looking for a new definition of their ethnicity; an ethnicity that transcends religion and creates a bond between all members of their culture, regardless of internal differences and, above all, regardless of the traditional hierarchical relations.

## 2.     Religion, traditional moral values and the transfer of tradition

### 2.1.   *The role of the priests in the ethnic transfer*

Ethnicity and religion of the *Suryoye* are closely interlinked. The preservation of religion and religion as a marker of the community are recurring themes. Separately or together, the religious and ethnic identity can strongly underpin communities (Smith 1991:8). Studying the Diaspora offers a key to understanding how a persistent religious singularity and an ethnic identity can form an inseparable identity complex (see Armstrong 1982:238). Even in present-day society, this strong ethno-religious identity complex continues to rival with an ethno-linguistic identity.

Religion plays a crucial part in transferring the myths of origin of an ethnic group[4]. Ethnic myths are often preserved via religious channels (Stallaert 1993:30). Organised religion, with its Holy Scripture, its liturgy, its fixed rituals and its clergy, is an important institution with regard to the preservation of ethnic societies. The 'myth of the chosen people', the holy texts and the prestige of the clergy are the framework wherein the traditions can survive for generations (Smith 1991:62). Smith notes that the priests are usually the guards of the ethnic border (Smith 1986:35). They also play an important role in the transfer of a 'myth-symbol complex'.

In pre-modern communities it is the priests, scribes and bards, often organized into guilds and castes, who recount, re-enact and codify traditions. Often as the only literate strata, and being necessary for intercession with divine forces, priests, scribes and bards achieve considerable influence and prestige in many communities (...)
Even in diaspora communities we find the priests, rabbis and doctors of law, organized along more or less centralized lines, forming an encompassing network of tribunals and counsel, and endowing far-flung enclaves with religious, legal and cultural unity in the face of the hostile environment. (...) religious officials and institutions were able to ensure the subjective unity and survival of the community and its historical and religious traditions (Smith 1991:38).

The *Suryoye* too look upon religion as a guard of tradition (and thus of the own identity) and as a safeguard against modernization.

In the first years after their arrival in Western Europe, the *Suryoye* did not organize any cultural or religious activities. The first parish was founded in 1971 in Augsburg (Germany) by priest Bitris Ogünc, who hailed from Midyat and had immigrated to Germany as a foreign worker (Sümer 1982:122). Until 1975, he was the only priest of the Syrian Orthodox Church in Germany, Switzerland, Belgium and the Netherlands. To this very day, he occupies an important position. He writes letters to every single parish, so that bonds remain strong.

Since 1975, the number of religious leaders has grown continuously. Thanks to the setting up in 1977 of a diocese for Central Europe and the Benelux in Hengelo (the Netherlands), the activities of the different congregations are now co-ordinated. Most of the priests are essentially migrants who, together with other people of their community, fled the unbearable situation in Southeast Turkey. Their appointment as a priest in Western Europe was not foreseen. Most of them merely underwent basic training for priesthood so that they could lead liturgical ceremonies, and their knowledge of the religious doctrine is therefore rather limited.

In the 19th century, Syrian Catholic seminars were strictly supervised by the Vatican, while the training of the Syrian Orthodox priests was lagging behind. The poor training of these priests is, until today, very clearly felt in the diaspora communities, where tradition is accepted uncritically as the answer to the problems of secularization and contacts with Western society. Nevertheless, traditions and values which are propagated by the community through the priests appear to form a stumbling block in the eyes of some of the youngsters.

The orthodoxy of religious values is measured by the orthodoxy of family values: Family life is thought to reflect how successfully religious values have been transferred. Notions of 'purity', 'impurity' and 'virtue' have a cultural content that is closely linked with the community's religious organization and is passed on to children at a very early age[5]. The transfer of ethnicity via the Church coincides with 'ethnic socialisation'.

The attitude of the *Suryoye* towards their priests is essentially traditional; they respectfully kiss the priest's hand, invite him into their homes, and offer him the place of honour at their tables. The traditional values are crucial for the survival of the community, and this is guaranteed by their religion. On the other hand, there is matter of loyalty to the Occidental host country of which one wants to become a citizen and in which one's children will have to find their place.

"For every problem that we encounter, we go and see the priest. First we discuss the problem with the priest and we take further steps together. The community had asked for a second priest. But the two priests don't get along at all. So now the community is divided: Some go and see the one priest, others prefer the second. But the priests must celebrate Mass together. It won't last though. Probably, the priest who arrived here last will be transferred, and someone new will be appointed, because we do need someone. The other priest seems to appreciate people whom he has known for some time, but when you first meet him he seems cold and reserved. I visited him once, and wanted to kiss his hand, out of respect and because that's what everybody else does. But he drew his hand back" (F.E., 24 yrs.).

Tradition serves as the answer to the confrontation with individualistic Western society. The singularity and the significance of a long and historically important tradition are strongly emphasized. If the younger generation complains or a compromise is sought between tradition and assimilation, the heads of the senior families rise with all their authority. Usually the priest is also the head of an important family and therefore has an interest in maintaining the traditional hierarchical structure. The traditionally theocratic structure, in which the patriarch is the figure of highest authority and the bishops are the judges, has to protect the ethnic borders against external influences in Occidental cities.

In the conflict between parents and their children, the parents usually follow the advice of the church leaders, who themselves have yet to find the answers to many conflicts between old and new values.

## 2.2. *The relation to the Occident and moral values*

### 2.2.1. 'Civilized' versus 'uncivilized'

On 1 and 2 October 1994, the German branch of the Assyrian Democratic Organisation (A.D.O.) held a weekend workshop about the conflict between traditional and modern values. The workshop was organized on request of the local sections of Gütersloh and Paderborn and under the auspices of the German and Middle European section of the A.D.O.[6]. At this conference, the sociologist Sabo Celik gave a lecture in which he asserted that 'anyone who wants to be politically active must first have a thorough knowledge of the history of his own people'. Celik believes that the family takes a central position in everyday village life. He notes that there is a hierarchical structure with a feudal *agha* at the top, a priest immediately below, and a family head below that. These three leading figures have firm control over the community, and everybody must show them respect. There is no democracy, but there is unity and solidarity.

In his speech Celik emphasized the difference between villages and cities, where leadership is less concentrated:

'Now people think: If we have to give something then we want something in return. Self-interest comes first in the towns, unlike in the villages. The more our people are oppressed, the richer they want to become in order to command consideration. In the towns, self-interest comes first. The youngsters are now trying to create unity. They have more options in towns. They are introduced to notions like democracy. But the danger of anonymity (assimilation) also increases'.

Two elements are striking here. On the one hand, the individual has become less important to the group and vice versa; there is, in other words, less solidarity. On the other hand, there is a greater sense of representation; there is, in other words, more democracy. This transition from solidarity to democracy coincides with a transition from a rural to an urban society, and this process is equated to assimilation.

Generally speaking, city-dwellers look upon themselves as *bajari* (civilized), while the villagers are labelled as *kurmanc* (uncivilized). Many villagers, for their part, consider the *bajariye* -despite their economic status- to be morally corrupted, egoistic and untrustworthy, even for their own family. However, these mutual conceptions are relative. The Midyoye (people from Midyat), for example, adopt the same attitude towards the Diyarbakri (people from Diarbakir). On the other hand, even the *bajariye* from such big Turkish cities as Diarbakir and Istanbul reject Occidental ideas, which are *bajari*-ideas par excellence. They are in turn regarded as *kurmanc* by those living in Western cities.

Clearly the distinction that is made between *bajari* and *kurmanc* is of a different nature than the ethnic dichotomy between Christians and Muslims. This explains why, despite their self-attributed status of *bajari*, so few marriages take place between members of the diaspora community and natives of their Occidental host countries. The issue of mixed marriages gives rise to recurring questions: According to which tradition will the children be educated? How will the own family be treated? etc.

The dichotomy between the own community's traditional values and Occidental values is a sensitive issue. Even if *Suryoye* appear to tend towards assimilation, they will generally avoid discussions about this particular subject.
Or they will place it in a broader context to try and prove their moral superiority.

This is exemplified by a conversation we had with M., a young Assyrian male from Hassana who is now living in a provincial town in Belgium.
He studies at university, and speaks fluent Dutch and French. M. says that he is willing to assimilate into Belgian society, but that he cannot accept its moral decay. By way of illustration, he told us the following story: M. used to have an old Belgian neighbour. One day the man died. His wife immediately telephoned her two sons to inform them of their father's death. The eldest son, a businessman, told her that it was difficult for him to come and see her on that particular day, because it would require him to cancel a number of appointments.

So he said that he would come over the next evening. According to M., the son's attitude was typical of the difference between the two communities. To a Suryoye, nothing could possibly be so important as to prevent him from immediately going to see his dead father and comfort his grieving mother. M. points out that at such moments the family is very important to Suryoye, while Belgians give priority to their job and to economic considerations. A couple of Belgian women who had been following the conversation did not agree with him. They argued that this kind of behaviour is not typical of Belgians at all and that the example was badly chosen. They went on to argue that Belgians too find their families important. M. did not reply to this.

The division between 'civilized' and 'uncivilized', which is believed to concur with a division between moral corruption and moral superiority, is a very ambivalent division. Being 'civilized' is economically attractive, but at the same time one wishes to retain or emphasize one's moral superiority. It is no coincidence that, in Southeast Turkey, the term for a countryman (*kurmandjiye*) is also used to refer to Kurds.

In migration, the complexity of the division is even greater. It is not only determined by the position one adopts with regard to the host country, but also by the relatives which one has left behind in the East: They will make sure that their kin in the Occident maintain family ties and thus remain *kurmanc*.

### 2.2.2. *One latno Suryeyto*? Am I not a Christian like you?

The relationship between *Suryoye* and non-*Suryoye* is the context for the construction of ethnicity. It is the proximity of the other which makes it necessary to demarcate one's own identity. A number of elements take a central position in the ethnic demarcation of the *Suryoye*:

- the ambivalent attitude towards the inhabitants of the host country (in this case: Belgium);
- the emphasis that is put on their not being Muslim;
- the emphasis that is put on their belonging to the first Christian Church.

The significance of 'Belgium' is not the same for the *Suryoye* as for those who recognize themselves as Belgians. It is asserted that Belgians are, first and foremost, Christians like the *Suryoye* are, but Belgians are also very *bajariye*, i.e. morally corrupted and not attached to family life. The positive side of the status of *bajariye* is the economic prestige that it entails. The *Suryoye* realize that these two factors are actually connected. Belgium as 'the land of milk and honey' is slowly resulting in the fragmentation of extended families into nuclear families.

On the whole, the *Suryoye* in Belgium are eager to make a distinction between themselves and the Turkish community in their host country. The following utterances are typical of this attitude:

"We are not immigrants who came here to earn money; we have come to live here, and our children will become Belgians'. 'We are not Turks; people call us Turks or they take us for filthy foreigners. But we're not just any foreigners. We want to become Belgians. One shouldn't simply equate us with foreign workers".

Many of these people came to Belgium assuming that they would finally be able to lead a quiet life in a 'Christian' country, instead of living between Muslims in a predominantly Islamic country. After a certain period of time, a part of the population comes to realize with a shock that Belgium is not a Christian country in the same way as Turkey is an Islamic country. Nevertheless, a large group does try to adhere to the criterion of ethnic division which the community has been applying for generations, i.e. religion. This group actually tries to be more 'Christian' that the Belgian Catholics. They will, for instance, point out that, unlike many Belgian Catholics, they go to church on Sundays so that at least their churches are full. Also typical of this point of view is the following statement made by a *Suryoyo* priest in Brussels:

"We left everything behind. The people who are still over there have little or no money, or they are unable to obtain a visa. And there's no sense in travelling illegally, because recently the Austrian government sent back Turkish Christians who'd tried that. Anyway, for us there is no country we could possibly return to. We'll just have to stay here, and the Belgian state must understand that we are doing our utmost to integrate. Let our children become Belgian children. The only thing we want to preserve is our way of life, because it's more

in keeping with the teachings of Jesus. Divorce, for instance, was unknown to us before, but by coming to live here we have been confronted with such problems.
We were taught to respect our father and those who are wiser. The education of our children is very important. The mutual respect between the parents is also important, and so is respect for one's elders. These values would be lost if we would allow them to be assimilated into Belgian society. That's why we must be permitted to live together as a group. So why are the newcomers not allowed to register in the municipalities where we live? Now, the authorities distribute them over numerous towns and villages. They will get lost here in Belgium and after a while they will merge into the existing structures. Here with us, in one group, we would be able to take care of them, arrange things for them, and they could always fall back on the community. We do want to integrate because this has become our country, but we also want to preserve the teachings of Jesus Christ" (Priest G. in Brussels, in an interview).

It is underlined that being a Christian is a system of moral values which has, however, lost its meaning in Belgian society.

The *Suryoye* are proud of their history and of the fact that their forefathers belonged to the first evangelized community. They forcefully assert that Christianity was not brought to them by missionaries like in many other countries of the world. Their Church is the cradle of the Latin Churches. Another aspect that is emphasized is that their language today is the same language as Jesus used to speak, unlike the languages of the Latin Churches which therefore do not have direct access to the word of Christ.

Many of these people, who had assumed that they were coming to a Christian country, are astonished by the size of the Turkish community in Belgium, often living in the same areas of the same towns as they are. They wonder why it is that some Christians are refused a residence permit, while so many Muslims are allowed to stay here. They also wonder why no distinction is made in Belgium between Muslim and Christian immigrants, and both groups are simply labelled as 'Turks'.

The confrontation with Belgian society has thus given rise to new questions. And it is in response to these questions that a new ethnicity is constructed. However, of central importance to this new ethnic identity the dichotomy between

Muslims and Christians remains; a dichotomy which, in turn, is deeply embedded in history. After all, the term *Suryoye* in its original sense meant 'we are Syrians', and in its broader sense it refers to the community which was first evangelized. However, living alongside the *Suryoye* in Southeast Turkey, there were also the *Tayye*, i.e. the Muslims.

Clearly, the new context in which the diaspora *Suryoye* are now living will also affect their consciousness as a group, as will be discussed later on. But first, we will deal with the question of language as an ethnic marker.

## 3.     Language as one of the markers of the ethnic identity

### 3.1.     *Language and ethnicity*

In a modern pluralistic society of a laic type, language is an outstanding criterion of identity; in the pre-modern era this relation used to be quite different, both in the Middle-East and in Europe. Though language sometimes had great symbolic significance for the identity, it was seldom the most important identification criterion[7]. Language and religion have always been very closely interwoven (for example, in missionary work), but only in a context where religious identification is the outstanding diacritic (Armstrong 1982: 243).

In migration, we notice a shift from a religious towards a cultural identification, whereby language becomes an important marker.

> It makes no difference how dissimilar members may be in their overt behaviour -if they say they are A, in contrast to another cognate category B, they are willing to be treated and let their behaviour be interpreted and judged as A's and not as B's (Barth 1969: 15).

In such a context language also becomes important as a 'border guard'. Armstrong asserts that the concept of linguistic codes is closely linked with the 'myth-symbol complex'. To speak a 'holy language' appears to be an important part of the (revised) *'mythomoteur'* (Armstrong 1982: 245). But the language situation among the *Suryoye* is very complex...

## 3.2. *Ethnographic aspects and the position of Ktobonoyo language*

To 'speak the language of Christ' is an ethnic demarcation with an extremely symbolic content.

> Unfortunately, nowadays, our language, the language of Christ and of the greatest people of old appears to be forgotten and lost. (...) Now, we ask you, Sons of Aram, to remember from which people you descend; to recall the greatness and the glory of your ancestors. We ask you to remain faithful to your language, the title of your honour, the reason of your existence and your history, invaluable treasure which you have inherited from your ancestors.
>
> (P. Al Khoury, Al Kafarnissy (s.d): 3. Translated from French).

Old Syrian language teaching mainly reaches the second generation. And this language revival is noticeable throughout Europe. The first generation was not so much interested in the cultural heritage as in a quick economic integration, with a preservation of the traditional religious hierarchy.

The following quote (1994) comes from a person who worked with the community during several years and who mainly dedicated himself to helping the first generation immigrants:

> "They value their own culture and their own religion, but there is no real tradition of scholarship, of seminars, of education amongst this Syrian Orthodox community. They seem to believe there is no need for all that. I have built up this entire library so that they could learn about the importance of their own language, their own religion, but nobody ever comes here, except for one or two individuals. You can become a Syrian Orthodox priest after only three weeks of training!!! At best these priests will learn a few stories and fables, which are systematically repeated during worship. There is no interest whatsoever for acquiring knowledge about their own religion, even though it is mentioned all the time. The status of the priest is very convenient to the *agha*, the traditional leader who must be honoured."

The second generation, for their part, are looking for new avenues, which they partly find in their own culture and to some extent in their language. About 5 years ago, a Suryoyo-Dutch dictionary was published[8].

However, the notion of their 'own language and culture' is not entirely unequivocal. The spoken language is essentially one of the Neo-Aramaic dialects, viz. Turoyo or Sureth. Some people, however, speak Kurdish, Turkish or Arabic.

In the third century AD, East Syrian became a cultivated language. It was also adopted as the liturgical language of the Syrian Christians and has retained this status ever since. This language was called *Suryoyo* (Syrian). Later, a distinction was made between *Suryoyo* as the vernacular and *Ktobonoyo* (the language of the Book). Notwithstanding the division of the Church, *Ktobonoyo* was retained as the common language, even though it was written according to three different alphabets. Meanwhile, the vernacular *Suryoyo* has undergone numerous linguistic developments.

East Syrian (usually referred to as Neo-Syrian) or *Aturaya* is the language which was spoken in Hakkari and in the district of Urmiah. The population has long since left Hakkari and now lives in Russia, Iraq, Syria and in the West.

Central Neo-Syrian is called *Sureth*. This dialect was mainly spoken by the Chaldeans and the Nestorians in Bothan in Southeast Turkey. The most widely known village where *Sureth* was spoken is Hassana. Several families from there are now living in Mechelen, a Belgian provincial town. This dialect is also spoken in Northern Iraq and in Iranian Azerbaijan. *Sureth* and *Aturaya* are cognate languages.

West Neo-Syrian is called *Turoyo* or *Suryoyo*. This language is spoken in Tur'Abdin. *Turoyo* and *Aturaya* are very different, and speakers of these two distinct languages can only partly understand each other.

These linguistic developments were influenced by other, surrounding languages: By Arabic and Kurdish, for instance, but also by Turkish and Persian. Consequently the differences between standard *Ktobonoyo* and the Neo-Syrian Dialects are very considerable. For example, Ritter (1967, see Björklund 1981:168) has ascertained that *Turoyo* contains more verbs of Arabic origin than verbs of Syrian origin.

The distinction between the languages does not only reflect a division within Syrian culture. The two Aramaic dialects still spoken today correspond with two denominations within the Church: Followers of the Syrian Orthodox Church speak West Syrian (*Suryoyo or Turoyo*), while followers of the Chaldean Church speak East Syrian (*Sureth and Aturaya*).

But classical Syrian (*Ktobonoyo*) is still the liturgical language of the Syrian Orthodox community, the Assyrians, the Chaldeans and the Maronites. It is precisely this shared language, this 'holy mother tongue', and not the vernacular, which is cultivated by the diaspora communities. *Ktobonoyo* has become the language of prestige which is taught in Church and in Sunday school. It is regarded as 'the language of Jesus', the language of intellectuals, the language of a rich and prestigious past. In fact there is an important distinction between, on the one hand, the Jews, Muslims and Orthodox communities, who still use an original liturgical language, and, on the other, the Christians who replaced Aramaic by Greek, then Latin and eventually the different native languages (Arkoun 1992(1989):49). The *Suryoye* use this as an argument to prove the link between Occidental Christianity and their own history, which is still relevant today. The myth of the unity of the community through a language with a prestigious and glorious past has today, in an age of migration to an Occidental country that is 'Christian' yet pluralistic, become an important element in the ethnic debate.

## 4. Religion, "objective" history and ethnicity of the Suryoye

### 4.1. *History and ethnicity*

The construction of ethnicity happens in relation to 'the other'; as a confrontation between how the community is looked upon by others and how it is perceived by its own members (see, among others, Barth 1969; Van den Berghe 1981; Katzir 1982).

In migration, this relation with 'the other' is basically the relation with the people of the Occident, which in this particular instance are Belgians. The question thus arises whether it is actually worthwhile to add a historical perspective. Is it not sufficient to define ethnicity in relation to the community's current social and political circumstances?

Several authors point out that it is important to study ethnic identification over a long period of time (De Vos 1975; Armstrong 1982; Smith 1982; Stallaert 1993). This approach allows one to compare the changes that may have occurred in the way in which a community defines itself as different contacts are established in different eras. The historical evolution which an ethnic identity undergoes will inevitably result in a complex framework with multifarious meanings. With regard to the *Suryoye*, this historical ambivalence continues to play a role in the controversy over the interpretation of ethnicity. In the case of a minority community, the identity appears to be defined by the contacts with the surrounding majority group as well as the own community's past. As the surrounding majority group in migration is perceived as 'the other', the question of identity arises in a situation of confrontation. Clearly, this confrontation with a new majority will result in a shift in the historically determined positioning of an ethnic group.

The division between the Suryoyo Christian Churches can only be understood as a continuous process if it is placed in a broader historical context. These Churches adhere to their own religious identity and, at the same time, they try to transcend this internal religious division in their confrontation with Occidental laicism by referring to a common past.

People structure and restructure significant relations in the light of new goals, problems and desires (Dolgin 1977:32). This is an active process involving whatever material is available, i.e. the previously formed meanings which present themselves within a new context. In the case of the *Suryoye*, the most important contrasting group during many centuries were in fact the Muslims. As such, the Muslims were important in defining the limits of their own civilization, in the same way as ethnic groups will contrast themselves with their neighbours. The relation with 'the other' was, in the eyes of the Christians of Southeast Turkey, essentially determined by a certain group of Muslims amongst whom they actually lived. These muslims in Turkish Kurdistan are mainly Kurds.

In a nutshell, we may conclude that the following three elements are important in the construction of the *Suryoyo* identity: The dichotomy between Islam and Christendom, the hierarchical structure of Kurdish social life, and the fragmentation of the Christian Church with its specific socio-cultural self-perception.

The age-old dichotomy between Islam and Christendom resulted in a certain mechanism with regard to the positioning of the *Suryoye* that is a perpetual process of integration and segregation.

## 4.2. *A continuous process of integration and segregation*

The *Suryoyo* community has existed as an ethnic minority for over 2000 years. This community (like for example the Armenians and the Jews) has preserved a very particular ethno-religious identity, even after a Diaspora across Europe and the Middle-East. It is the type of society where an anthropological reading of academic historiography can lead to an understanding of historically determined social models regarding membership of the community as well as relations with other communities.

The boundaries between the own group and 'the others' are repeatedly redefined through mechanisms of assimilation and segregation, both internally and externally (Katzir 1982:266). The ethnogenesis of the *Suryoye* shows that there is a continuous interaction between internal and external pressure to assimilate (i.e. an integration mechanism): External pressure to convert to Islam, for example, and an internal impulse to integrate in political, economic and cultural life of an essentially Islamic community. This integration mechanism coincides with a segregation mechanism, which can also be either internal or external. Examples of external segregation are the fact that members of the Christian communities were subject to a different tax system, had little chance of marrying outside the group, etc... Besides such mechanisms of external segregation there are mechanisms of internal segregation which emphasize the differences with the surrounding groups, even when the community is under severe pressure to assimilate, and perhaps even as a result of a certain degree of assimilation into the outside world.

This constant confrontation between the own community and 'the others', who are socially and politically more powerful, has created models for ethnic survival as a minority group. Throughout history, the group has retained its 'holy' language, its religion, and its ethnic identity, and it has done so in a situation of confrontation with the other communities. On the other hand, the surrounding majority groups of the past provided principles of social organisation which, within the new context of a different society (e.g. Brussels), can become useful, albeit temporarily, as ethnic markers.

* The socio-cultural self-perception of the Churches

The Christians of ancient Mesopotamia had already been evangelized during the first century, but from 400 AD onwards they were divided in a fierce theological dispute. In simplified terms, one could say that there were two movements in the Byzantine Empire: The one was pro-Byzantine and the other was an opposition movement which found expression in matters of religion. The Pro-Byzantine movement was Greek Orthodox, while the opposition was divided into a Coptic Church (mainly in Egypt), and a Nestorian and a Syrian Orthodox Church (both rooted in *Suryoyo* culture). Soon after, there was a division into an East Syrian and a West Syrian Church. The East Syrian Church adhered to the line of the Church Father Nestorius and consequently its disciples were called Nestorians (or Assyrians, by the British). The West Syrian Church was named the Jacobite Church, after Jacobus Baradeus, and its disciples were Syrian Orthodox. The Greek Orthodox Church too originates in the West Syrian Church.

Scholars of these early Christian Churches sometimes debate the ethnic implications of these differences (Armstrong 1982:204).

In the theological writings of Severus of Antioch (the Syrian Orthodox Church) a culturally important issue is discussed: How to attain security through economic and material well-being as a gift of God. This concept took on a particular significance in the confrontation with Islam: By applying themselves to trade, Christians could find compensation for their exclusion from other professions, including public office. Furthermore, their material well-being was further enhanced by the '*dzimmi-status*', whereby protection and safety were offered in exchange for the payment of a tax.

In the theology of the Nestorians, on the other hand, central importance is attributed to obedience and worship. In the confrontation with Islam, this element too is interpreted in a particular way. The emphasis lies on the human feelings with regard to concrete mysteries, supported by a Resurrection theology. The notion of 'resurrection' is interpreted quite materially. Mystery is reduced to miracle; an idea which is also present in the Syrian Orthodox religion, because man, the temple of God, is holy. This leads to a very subjective and physical interpretation of a resurrection, which also finds expression in the ethnic reading of history. Relations of superiority and inferiority can alternate constantly. In recent history, for example, some Nestorians fled to Baghdad, while others travelled to Chicago. And both groups proceeded from a materialistic interpretation of what the notion of 'resurrection' might imply for them.

It is engraved on the collective memory of both Nestorians as the Syrian Orthodox Christians that they once belonged to a majority group, and this is significant for their current strategies of ethnic demarcation in the diaspora. The notion of 'having once belonged to a majority group' is accompanied by the realization that today, in this situation of migration, they once again belong to a religious majority. Since Islamic rule over Turkey, they were increasingly isolated as a shrinking minority group, a process that was further enhanced by the anti-minorities policies that have been pursued since the era of Atatürk.

The ambition to break out of this inferior, isolated position is still alive today, and they see two ways of accomplishing this in their migratory existence. On the one hand, they will try to establish themselves as being 'morally superior' to the (secular) Occident, by transcending their own religious division and stressing the fact that they were once part of the great Assyrian Empire, the cradle of Occidental culture.
On the other hand, they will draw attention to their Christian religion and their language, which was the language of Christ, and emphasize that their original homeland was the cradle of all Christian Churches, including that of the West.

* The dichotomy between Islam and Christendom

Two elements are of central importance in the confrontation with Islam: Firstly, there is the continuous struggle between superiority and inferiority, which lies at the root of the social positioning of the *Suryoye*, both in their country of origin and in migration. A second factor is the ambivalent relation between the religious and the ethnic diacritic. History tells us that the struggle between superiority and inferiority has gradually shifted from an ethnic (Arabs versus non-Arabs) to a religious interpretation (Muslims versus non-Muslims) (Chabry 1987:33).

From the beginning, the concepts introduced by the emergence of Islam conflicted with the values of old Arabic society. One of the sources of this conflict lay in the status of individuals and the hierarchy between the different social categories. Islam wanted to introduce a new norm consisting of just one distinguishing principle between individuals, i.e. their religion. Not only did this imply that all Muslims were superior to non-Muslims, but it also meant that Muslims were equals, regardless of their social position or ethnic origin (Gardet 1961:213). Islam did, in fact, introduce a universal, non-racist, non-tribal view of relations between believers (Platti, 1995:100). According to Islamic values, the criterion of equality is the Muslim faith. According to Arabic values, by contrast, the criterion is being Arab (Gardet 1961:213 en Platti 1995:93).

This element of tension between the religious criterion and the ethnic criterion, which was evident from the very first confrontation with Islam, would later prove to be of great significance to the creation of ethnic communities.

The Christians were, from the very first confrontation, granted the status of *dzimmi*: They are protected, yet inferior. The Arab Christians try to find a way out of this position by emphasizing the ethnic criterion (Chabry 1987: 332).

After the crusades, the attitude of the Muslims towards the Christians changed dramatically. The Muslim world had come to realise that the Christians could also turn against Islam. As far as they were concerned, the Christians had transformed into a potentially hostile group; a clear example of an ethnic categorization that is replaced by a religious one (Valognes 1994).

The Christians of the Middle East, for their part, were regarded by the crusaders as *'Christians in name only'* (Le Goff 1987 (1984):177). The rather hostile and ambivalent attitude that was adopted towards these Christians was the consequence of the schism that had occurred in the 4th century AD and which, over the centuries, had developed into an unbridgeable gap: 'The incomprehension had slowly developed into hatred, daughter of ignorance. The

Latins felt towards the Greeks a mixture of envy and disgust, the result of a more or less repressed sense of inferiority' (Le Goff 1987 (1984): 177).

The Christians of the Middle East were thus confronted with two kinds of contempt: The contempt shown by the Muslims, as a consequence of a sense of superiority, and the contempt of the Latin Christians, resulting from a feeling of inferiority.

With the rise of the Ottoman Empire, the subdivision of the territory came to be based on the criterion of religion. The Islamic, Christian, and Jewish communities (the so-called *millets*) were segregated from each other. The *millet* system, which resulted in a shift from ethno-religious categories to ethnic communities, contributed to the rigidity of the traditions of each of the groups. As a result of the zealous missionary work on the part of the Catholics and Protestants since the end of the 16th century, the process of ethnic division was further accelerated. People tried to elude the *dzimmi* status by emphasizing the bonds with the larger Occidental Christian community.

* The *dzimmi*-status and isolation as important external factors in the preservation of the ethnic group

There preservation of the ethnic identity over such a long period of time was made possible by two contributing external factors: (i) the geographical and cultural isolation and (ii) the *dzimmi*-status.

After the invasion of the Mongols in 1258 AD, the Christians were vehemently persecuted. As a consequence, the Syrian Orthodox Christians withdrew to their traditional homeland: The mountains of *Tur`Abdin*. The Nestorians, for their part, fled persecution by Timur (1393), and retreated to the mountainous region of *Hakkari* in Kurdistan. There they reorganised themselves on a tribal basis. Gradually, certain towns and villages in Southeast Turkey became the homeland of the *Suryoye*, entailing that the *Suryoyo* community had to sustain itself almost exclusively within a Kurdish society. Their geographical and cultural isolation led to a co-existence with the Kurds and a relative integration into the Kurdish tribal system.

It also resulted in social and cultural activities of the *Suryoye* predominantly taking place within the context of small Christian patrilineal communities and enlarged families.

\* The assimilation of elements of Kurdish culture

Until today, the Muslims with whom the Christians of Southeast Turkey have contact are mainly Kurds. The conflict of values, inherent in the confrontation between Muslims and Christians, was further intensified by the specific tribal relations of the Kurds, with Christians usually adopting an inferior position towards a Kurdish *Agha* to increase their own safety.

The Christians paid an extra tax and, in return, they became part of the local Kurdish tribal system, whereby they usually received protection from the local chieftains. In Kurdish tribal society, salesmen and craftsmen had a low status. By applying themselves to these professions, the Christians constructed an economic system that isolated them as a community but, at the same time, integrated them in a larger economic framework. Gold- and silversmithery and the clothing industry are still important economic components of Aramaic-Christian society.

Eventually, the Christians started to have *aghas* of their own and they increasingly assimilated the specific Kurdish tribal structure. An important aspect with regard to the *Suryoyo* groups in the assimilation of certain Kurdish elements is the fact that the tribal sections were strongly endogamous.

Another important aspect is the close connection between leadership and conflict: In establishing one's authority, it is not so much one's ability to control conflicts, but the ability to cause and resolve conflicts that is thought to be significant. Two elements are important with regard to the *agha*: He is the intermediary between the community and the outside world, and the villagers donate him part of their income.

4.3.    *The process of expulsion and the new ethnic positioning in Western Europe*

By 1924, few Assyrians were still living in Turkey. Most had already fled to Northern Iraq. They were helped in their flight by the British army, and placed in camps in Babouka, Mossoul, Dohuk and Amadya. 1924 and 1925 were extremely difficult years for the Christians. They were driven out of the *Tur'Abdin* mountains and the Syrian patriarch was dethroned. While Agha Petros, who had fled, was leading a provisional government of the Assyro-Chaldean Republic, the remaining Assyrians in Iraq were fighting for their rights. After the end of the British mandate (1932) and the assumption of power by the ultra-nationalist party (the National Brotherhood), the Assyrians were left to fend for themselves. In August of 1933, the Assyrians were massacred throughout the province of Mossoul[9].

The exodus, which had already begun in 1915, continued between the two World Wars, mainly to the French mandates of Syria and Lebanon.

Lebanon was a favourite country for emigration; it was attractive because of the economic possibilities it offered and because its society was religiously balanced. President Chamoun[10], who was himself a Christian, had followed a pro-Western policy and was not popular among the Muslim population, which had strong Pan-Arabic feelings. Riots broke out, and the U.S. decided to intervene militarily. Since these events, it has become virtually impossible for members of the Syrian Orthodox community to acquire Lebanese nationality. But these difficulties did not stem the flow immigration, which actually continued until the outbreak of the Lebanese civil war.

Then there was the Cyprus crisis (1963-1974) which further jeopardized the position of the Christians in Turkey. Soon after the Turkish military intervention of 1974 had restored order on the island, the jubilant mood in Turkey turned against the Christians. This prompted many Christians to emigrate to Western Europe, initially as guest workers and later, after the implementation of an immigration stop, as asylum seekers. It is estimated that over 160,000 Christians came to Western Europe in this migratory movement (Study group Middle East 1983: 8).

With the civil war in Lebanon (1974-1977) many Kurds resettled in Southeast Turkey. Their return to the region has become one of the principal causes of renewed aggression against the Christians.

The coup of 1980 resulted in a deterioration of the situation in the villages. In a report dating from 1982[11], the Council of Europe describes a whole series of attacks on Christians: The looting of the *Mar Melki* monastery in Midyat by a group of armed Muslims, murders and theft in Hassana (Djérizeh)... The situation in cities was reported to be less volatile: Christians appeared to be safer there.

But since the coup, the problem of the Kurds in the villages of Southeast Turkey has also been accentuated. Contrary to most Christians, the Kurds had not been given separate protection under the Treaty of Lausanne (1923). A few years after this treaty, the government in Ankara launched a campaign of violence against the Kurds. The Turkish government embarked on a policy of systematic Turkification, whereby the Kurdish identity was simply ignored. But the repression has, especially after the 1980 coup, stimulated the emergence of a radical guerilla movement, i.e. the Kurdish Workers Party (P.K.K.). Fighting in Kurdistan has not ceased since, and the pressure on Christian villages in Southeast Turkey has further increased.

The *Suryoye*, for that matter, were also 'overlooked' by the Treaty of Lausanne, as a result of which they still do not enjoy any legal protection as cultural minority. Although this was apparently not the intention of the treaty, it has become the interpretation given to it by the Turkish authorities. At any time can their schools, hospitals and churches be closed by Turkish authorities, and indeed this has already happened. One in four churches in the province of Mardin have been closed since 1978. While the Syrian Orthodox community was officially given permission to practise its religion, it was prohibited to teach the Syrian language and religious education had to take place in Turkish. It thus became virtually impossible to transmit the community's culture to the children, and consequently these children became increasingly 'Turkish'.

The *Suryoye* in Turkey are leaving their country in great numbers to try and build a new future elsewhere. But, in building their future, the *Suryoye* also look back to their past, though it does remain a subject of internal debate in exactly which direction this past lies.

## 5. Conclusion

The *Suryoye* manifest themselves as a cluster of closely interwoven communities who carry with them a long and complex past in which 'objective' and 'subjective' history are continuously interlinked; a mechanism that is nourished by myths about the earliest beginnings. From this has gradually emerged a movable and modulated matrix based on ethno-religious elements.

In the recent situation of migration, however, new processes of ethnic positioning have burgeoned, though these continue to be highly coloured by a past which the cluster cultivates in its closeness. Yet fresh impulses are made possible, induced even, by the new context of Western society.

It is this enormous complexity of myths, languages and stories, historically 'objective' and subjectively perceived developments in the past, coupled with newly created possibilities in migration, which we have compactly described in this contribution, focusing primarily on the construction of ethnicity from the past.

*Notes*

1.  The names *Suryoyo* and *Suryoye* are used alternately by the community itself so that there is not a clear distinction between the two.

2.  Like Armstrong, we shall use the term 'Christendom' to refer to Christian civilization, and the term 'Christianity' to refer to the Christian religion (Armstrong 1982: 308). However, the term 'Islam' may refer to either Islamic civilization or the religion.

3.  Patriarch Mor Ignatius Zakka I Iwas was born in 1933 in Mossul, Iraq. He was educated in Iraq at schools such as Al Tahtip and St Thomas, and went on to study theology at the Saint Afrem Institute. In 1960, he travelled to the U.S. to complete his theological studies. He later became secretary to both patriarch Afrem Barsom I and patriarch Yakkup III. On 17 November 1963 he was enthroned as bishop of Mousel in Iraq. He later became bishop of Baghdad, and on 11 July 1980 he was chosen as patriarch. The patriarch has the same significance to the Syrian Orthodox community as the pope has to the Catholics. See Shemso, Social, cultural and informative magazine, vol.9, no. 38, 1994.

4.  'There is no evidence that people's religious imagination has been reduced in modern, urban society. The contexts of belief or, better, the modalities of truth with which we approach these areas of the constitutive imagination may have changed, but the appeal of the old themes seems to have survived' (Joao de Pina-Cabral 1992: 56).

5.  De Vos sees a connection between the notions of purity and impurity in religion and the cultural content which is given to these notions (De Vos 1987:318). The dimension of purity and impurity is closely linked with the ethnic boundaries between the own community and the others (De Vos 1987: 319-320).

6.  For a report on this workshop, see Shemsho, Social, cultural and informative magazine, vol.9, no. 39, November 1994.

7.  During the Umayyad dynasty (661-750) and certainly during the Abbasid dynasty (750-1258), the language of conquered peoples was not adopted. Instead, the Arab conquerors insisted on the use of Arabic as the administrative language. Resistance to Arabic was equated with resistance to Islam. But within Islamic political life, there were soon two or more co-existing languages. The basic idea was that the holders of each of the three cultural and linguistic traditions could perform certain functions: Arabic for religious law, Persian for the central administration, and Turkish for the military sphere. The reigning elite was thus ethnically segmented (Armstrong 1982:245).

8.  This dictionary was compiled by Simon Ato from Enschede in the Netherlands.

9.  According to a report in the Geneva-based newspaper 'Journal de Genève' some 2,000 people were killed. The Assyrians claim there were 3,000 dead. (Wantoestand van de Assyrische minderheid in het Midden-Oosten, Droit de l'homme sans frontière, Braine-le-Comte, and the Assyrian Democratic Organization, Augsburg, 1994, p.25).

10. President from 1952 until 1958; assassinated in 1991.

11. Rapport de la commission juridique de l'Assembleé parlementaire du Conseil de l'Europe, Strassbourg, 1982, p.90.

# Chapter V:

# Ethnicity and Historicity in Transylvania

**Greet Van de Vyver**

## 1. Introduction

Transylvania is a region in Western Romania that borders Hungary in the West, the former Yugoslavia (Vojvodina) in the Southwest and the Ukraine in the North. The ethnic and religious composition of its population is more heterogeneous than that of the rest of Romania: While in the country's other regions, the Romanians[1] represent over 97 per cent of the overall population, their share in the overall population of Transylvania (approx. 7,500,000) amounts to only 71 per cent. Here, the remainder are primarily ethnic Hungarians (23 %)[2], but numerous other ethnic groups are also represented, including Roma, Germans, Ukrainians and Serbs (Recensàmîntul populatiei si locuintelor 1992: 14-25).

During fourteen months, in 1993, 1994 and 1995, I conducted anthropological fieldwork in three Transylvanian villages: Two ethnically mixed villages, Dumbrava and Mànàstireni, and one homogeneous Hungarian village called Inucu. All three are located in the province of Cluj. Half the inhabitants of Dumbrava are ethnic Hungarians, 30 per cent are ethnic Romanians and one fifth are Gypsies. In Mànàstireni, however, the situation is quite different: Here a 66 per cent majority is Romanian, while ethnic Hungarians make up just over a quarter of the population and the Gypsies are a minority comprising only six per cent of the inhabitants. In Inucu everyone is Hungarian. Ethnicity and religion coincide among the Romanian and Hungarian inhabitants of these villages. That is to say, the Romanians have the Orthodox faith whereas the ethnic Hungarians of Dumbrava, Mànàstireni and Inucu are Calvinist. The majority of the Gypsies are Orthodox, some are Calvinist but, on the whole, Gypsies are not regular churchgoers.

## 2. The traditional ethnic self-images

Every foreign visitor to Transylvania soon becomes aware of a preoccupation with issues of cultural and ethnic identity both at macro- and microlevel. In exploring the content of the people's perception of their own ethnic group and that of others, we can reach an understanding of the pattern of inter-ethnic relations which is characteristic of present-day social life in Transylvania. My view on the self-perception of the three main ethnic groups of this region -the ethnic Romanians, the ethnic Hungarians and the Gypsies -, is mainly based on examples drawn from my anthropological fieldwork in the villages mentioned.

### 2.1 *The traditional self-image of the Romanians*

Despite the fact that the ethnic Romanians make up the majority of Transylvania's population and their native tongue is the country's official language, the Romanian villagers see themselves as an ethnic group which, just like all the other ethnic communities, has to fight for its basic rights and for the preservation of its ethnic and cultural identity. The following utterances by Romanian villagers typify the identity which ethnic Romanians attribute to themselves:

"One day a rich Hungarian count came to check his serfs' work. He met Ioan Coldea and said to him: 'Just look what a beautiful country this is. And we have been living here for all of a thousand years! Of course, you (= Romanian people) can't say that, can you?' The farmer gave this some thought and answered 'No, we can't, because we have always lived here.'"

"Traditionally, Romanians are a very tolerant people who are not interested in territorial expansion, but who have suffered a lot because of the urge of other peoples to conquer and expand."

"We haven't become Christians, but were born as Christians. What's more, we defended Christianity with all our might and main against advancing Islam."

"Our people have a long history: We descend from the Dacians and the old Romans, and so we are Latin. Our language is related to French and Italian."

"Here, in our village, there's nothing worth studying. The real Romanian customs and traditions have survived in the mountain villages."

As is the case with other peoples of Eastern Europe, history and language are important to the Romanian self-image. Some features which may be broadly defined as basic elements of the Romanian self-perception are:

- their part-Roman, part-Dacian ancestry
- their being born as Christians
- their language being a Romance language

In fact, these three characteristics are closely related, for they all stem from the same historical myth[3] about their people's origin, also referred to as the Daco-Roman descent myth. According to this myth, there was, around the beginning of the Roman calendar, a well-organized people, the so-called Dacians, living in (what is now known as) Transylvania. They were conquered by the Romans under emperor Trajan in 106 AD, and their territory was made a Roman province. Subsequently, an intense amalgamation took place of the Dacians and the Romans and their respective cultures, resulting in the birth of the Romanian people, their language and their culture (Giurescu 1967: 16-34). The Romanian historian Stefan Pascu situates the completion of this process or 'ethnogenesis' in the eight century: The Daco-Roman population had become the Romanian people, and their language, so-called Vulgar Latin, had evolved into Romanian (Pascu 1982: 36).

This myth about the ancestors of the Romanians is deeply embedded in popular consciousness. The belief in their descent from the Romans entails that they consider themselves as an essentially European people. Romanians feel hurt, insulted even, when they notice that others in Western Europe hold a different view. Moreover, they see themselves as once having been a stronghold of Christianity and of western culture, having defended them against the savage peoples of Asia and against advancing Islam during many centuries.

The Hungarians are considered by a large part of the Romanian community as one of those barbaric peoples who, thanks to their ruthlessness, were able to settle for good in Transylvania from the eleventh century. The make-up of the ethnic identity of the Transylvanian Romanians cannot be detached from the presence of this ethnic group. On the contrary, it is partly determined by it. The Romanian community positions itself opposite the Hungarian ethnic group by attributing central importance to two elements in their self-image: Their continuous presence in Transylvania and the importance of the region as the cradle of their civilisation. The first element is known as the Romanian continuity theory[4]. According to this theory, the Romanians, who were descended from the romanised Dacians, withdrew to the Transylvanian plateau after the retreat of the Roman occupiers, where they subsequently preserved their Romance language and culture. It is claimed that they have lived uninterrupted in this region ever since (Giurescu 1967: 35-40; Istoria românilor 1994: 67).

This implies that they consider themselves as the oldest inhabitants of Transylvania, whereas the Hungarians are seen as 'newcomers' who conquered the region centuries later and settled there alongside the original Romanian inhabitants.

From this perspective, one can understand why the term *'bozgori'*, by which the Romanians address the Magyars, is considered unpleasant by the latter. The term *'bozgor'* means as much as 'you who came' and thus hints at the Romanian continuity theory according to which the Hungarian tribes arrived in Transylvania long after the Romanian people, who had been living there for hundreds of years.

Not only do the Romanians claim 'right of primogeniture' to Transylvania, but they also attach a mythical meaning to the mountainous region: It is their idealized homeland and the region which at certain points in history played a crucial part in the survival of the Romanian nation and culture. The close bond between the Romanian population and Transylvania is especially significant in the context of the co-existence with the ethnic Hungarians.

Another typical feature of the Romanian self-image is their sense of drive for unification which has manifested itself throughout the people's history (Schöpflin 1974: 87). This comprises the strong belief that there is, as it were, an inherent logic to their history, which led to the political unification of the historical regions of Transylvania, Walachia and Moldavia. The great importance that the Romanians attach to the unity of the country is, among other things, evident in the extreme pride they take in the Romanian language: Romanians proudly assert that regional variations are minor and in no way impede mutual communications, not even between inhabitants of the most distant areas.

The Gypsies' presence and their confrontation with the Romanian villagers is, on the other hand, of minor importance to the self-image of the latter group, especially in comparison with the influence of the ethnic Hungarians, but it nevertheless exists. Beck (1989: 53) points out that Gypsies played a role in the construction of the Romanian identity in the sense that all kinds of persistent prejudices against the Gypsy community were used to measure the qualities of the own Romanian culture. He goes on to explain that 'as the Tigani increasingly took on an ethnic and racial character, Romanians could increasingly identify themselves in contradiction to their low class status, a process that helped shape the Romanian national states and Romanian ethnic identity' (Beck 1989: 61).

## 2.2. *The traditional self-image of the Magyars*

The myth about Hunor and Magor, which is an idyllic representation of the birth of the Magyars and the Huns, is one of the best known myths among the Hungarian villagers, not least because it is taught at school in Hungarian language-classes[5].

Hunor and Magor, sons of king Nimrod, get utterly lost during a deerhunt. On their ensuing ramble, they discover a beautiful hidden country that is wild and fertile, and they decide to settle there. But during a closer exploration of the surrounding territory they stumble upon an encampment which is occupied merely by elderly people, women and children. The leader of the encampment Béliar and his warriors are absent. Subsequently, Hunor and Magor put the elderly to the sword, while the women and children are captured. But by coincidence, these prisoners include king Dula's two beautiful daughters who, at the side of their newly found masters, will each give birth to an entire people, viz. the Huns and the Magyars (Schipper 1992: 113-114)[6].

Most Hungarians are aware not so much of the myth's actual content as its underlying twofold message: The Hungarian kinship with the Huns and the mythical -and therefore unquestionable- appropriation of Transylvania to these peoples. Those two elements contribute to the Hungarian self-image. It is, however, striking that many Magyars do not only look upon themselves as being distant relatives of the Huns, but also as direct descendants of Attila's Hunnish warrior tribes.

The region of Transylvania is equally important to the self-perception of the rural ethnic Hungarians as it is to that of the Romanians. The Hungarians claim that their tribes, under the leadership of Arpad, son of Almos, crossed the Danube and the Carpathian Mountains in 895 AD to flee attacks, moving into Transylvania for the first time. They believe that, at the time of the Hungarian conquest, Transylvania was uninhabited or at most thinly populated by Slavonic tribes (Köpeczi 1994: 109-114). It is claimed by Hungarian historians that the romanised population of the Province of Dacia had fled the advancing barbarians to the area south of the Danube at the end of the third century. In their view, the Romanians are 'newcomers' in Transylvania, having migrated from their Balkan homeland in the thirteenth century. Hungarian historians maintain that the earliest mention of Transylvanian Romanians is in a historical document dating from 1222, in which they are referred to as groups of transhumant Vlach shepherds who were allowed by the Hungarian overlords to settle in their region (Köpeczi 1994: 183-191). So, the Hungarians too see Transylvania as their own, having settled there first and having lived there for more than two centuries before the arrival of the Romanians.

Furthermore, according to some Hungarian villagers, especially the lower social strata among them,Transylvania has safeguarded the historical continuity of Hungarian culture and the Hungarian state. Unlike mountainous regions as Transylvania, the greatest part of the Hungarian kingdom was a plain and consequently more easy to gain control over. In the collective Hungarian consciousness the only true Hungarians are those who lived in the mountains of Transylvania and preserved the genuine Hungarian culture in times of foreign occupation.

Both rural Hungarians and Romanians see themselves as the earliest inhabitants of Transylvania which some regard as the cradle of their civilization. Often, the question of 'the right of primogeniture' is accompanied by the claim for 'historical rights' to this region (Schöplin & Poulton 1990: 8).

All Magyars consider the Hungarian language as the basic symbol of their identity. But in the ethnic discourse of some Magyars, central importance is sooner attributed to religious and cultural features. They essentially perceive themselves as a Christian people and usually attach great significance to the potent myth of Saint Stephen, whom they see as their Christian apostolic king who in

1000 AD received a Holy Crown from the pope and consequently ruled through the grace of divine power. Furthermore, the Hungarians, belonging to the Christian community of the west, claim that they were once the shield of Christianity against Islam.

Most Hungarians view themselves as essentially 'European', while the Romanians are described as 'oriental' and 'lacking culture'. Or, as the sociologists Buckley and Nixon formulate it in a nutshell: 'Like the Romanian recourse to self-affirmation through the assumption that Roman blood runs in his veins, the Hungarian equivalent suggests that all of their group have the blood of the nobility' (Buckley and Nixon, 1998: 7). The ethnic Hungarians readily assert that the relative affluence of the inhabitants of Transylvania, in comparison with people in the rest of Romania, is largely due to the former Hungarian political and cultural policies and to the presence in this region of the diligent Hungarians and Germans. Gypsies do not seem to play a part in the ethnic discourse of the Magyars.

## 2.3. *The traditional self-image of the Gypsies*

'Noi suntem tigani, và spun sincer. Dar suntem romanisati. Noi suntem curati si noi lucràm. Suntem sàraci, dar lucràm'. (We are Gypsies; I frankly admit that. But we are 'romanianized'. We are clean and we work. We are poor but we work).

'Noi suntem tigani români dar vecinii nostri sunt tigani unguri'. (We are Romanian Gypsies but our neighbours are Hungarian Gypsies).

In contrast to what, by analogy with the two other ethnic groups, one might logically expect, history does not seem to play a significant role in the self-image of the Gypsies in the villages that I studied. In fact, they do not refer to the history of their people or any kind of homeland when describing their own identity. Myths of origin and descent are unknown to them.

Moreover, it appears that their own language, Tigàneste, which is still the colloquial language of many Gypsies in Dumbrava, is not relevant to their self-image either. Then what does their self-image consist of? There are two key elements: The image of Gypsies that prevails in the non-Gypsy community and, to a lesser degree, religion.

The stereotyped image of Gypsies as "an itinerant, uncivilised, lazy and unhygienic people, who live off begging and stealing, and breed like rabbits", is deeply rooted in the minds of most non-Gypsies. Characteristic of the Gypsies' self-image is that they emphasize exactly the opposite: They say that they have been sedentary for ages, are adapted or 'romanianized', clean, and as hard-working as the other inhabitants of the village. In fact, their self-image is the negation of the prejudice against them; an attempt to break through the stigmatisation. Some Gypsies even go so far as to conceal or deny their identity and present themselves as Romanians. Strikingly, this is even true of some Gypsy children.

When the issue of ethnic identity is raised, the Gypsies of Durmbrava and its environs divide their local ethnic community into two groups: the 'Romanian Gypsies' and the 'Hungarian Gypsies'.The distinction is not based on language but on religion; that is to say, on the actual church building in which they were baptized.

## 3. The current social inter-ethnic positioning

### 3.1. *The Romanians*

After the political revolution of 1989, a number of radical cultural 'reforms' were carried through in Romania which were the public expression of the Romanian people's consciousness of their Daco-Roman descent. Two remarkable examples are: the national anthem and the spelling of the Romanian language.

The present-day Romanian anthem *Desteaptà-te, Române*, is an old, but widely known folk song that was arranged in the 19th century by Andrei Muresianu. It is said that the Romanians often sung this song during the 1848 revolution. Its second stanza goes as follows:

Acum ori niciodatà sà dàm dovezi la lume cà-n aste mîini mai curge un sînge de roman si cà-n a noastre piepturi pàstràm cu falà-un nume triumfàtor în lupte, un nume de Traian! (Ràdulescu 1990).

Now or never shall we prove to the world that *Roman* blood runs through our hands, and that deep down in our hearts we proudly keep the name of a man victorious in battle, the name of *Trajan*[7].

The acceptance of this old folksong as the Romanian national anthem after Ceausescu's overthrow shows that the Daco-Roman descent is seen as the core of the Romanian nature.

During the Communist era, especially in the late 1940s and 1950s, Romanian culture was subjected to a process of denationalization which took the form of a sustained and far-reaching campaign of 'Slavicization'. One of the most striking features of this campaign was the resolution of the Council of Ministers on 16 September 1953 which provided the replacement of the letter â with î, the Romanian form of a character used in the Cyrillic alphabet of the Romanians until 1860. The Romanians experienced this orthographic change as particularly humiliating, as the very name of their people and their country was now to be spelt respectively romîni and Romînia instead of the etymologically-based români and România, which highlighted their Roman ancestry. Moreover, philologists emphasized the extensive Slavonic influence on the vocabulary and morphology of Romanian, and at school children were taught that Romanian was a Slavonic language with some superimposed neo-Latin elements.

The effort to obscure the Latin origin of the language can be explained as a concomitant of the drive by the Soviet Union to isolate their Romanian satellite completely from the West and Western influences by cutting the existing links with the West and by underlining historical and cultural affinities with Russia.

But it was not long before a reaction occurred. In the early 1960s the poet Tudor Arghezi called for a reinstatement of the letter â; a call which was partly answered: Its use in the name of the country and its people was officially reintroduced in the spring of 1965 (Schöpflin 1974: 84-87).

On 17 February 1993 the orthographic discussion was re-opened by the General Assembly of the Romanian Academy. The government approved their proposal and announced that henceforth the letter î was to be replaced with â, except when it is the initial letter of a word. It was also decided that in the present tense of the verb 'to be' (a fi) the letter u would be used instead of î (Draganescu 1993: 356-357)[8]. This 'new' spelling, which emphasizes the Latin character of Romanian language, was in fact a restoration of the previous orthography, which had been introduced in 1932.

The people's Daco-Roman ancestry is also evident in a number of everyday names, viz. the Romanian car *Dacia*, institutions like the *Dacia Felix Bank,* streetnames, hotels and towns like hotel *Hercules* in *Bàile Herculane* and *The hotel of the Emperor of the Romans* in Sibiu.

And all kinds of typical Dacian objects and/or relics of the Roman civilisation are exhibited in historical and ethnographic museums.

## 3.2. *The Magyars*

The Magyars' identity and the will to preserve it are expressed most clearly in their very strong attachment to the Magyar language. The ethnic Hungarians of Dumbrava, Mànàstireni and Inucu always speak Hungarian among each other, even in the presence of people who do not understand the language. They only use the Romanian language when directly addressing a non-Hungarian. They spend much of their leisure time listening to Radio Budapest, playing Hungarian songs, watching Hungarian-language television programmes, or reading Hungarian newspapers, magazines or books. Hungarian ministers play an important role in the preservation of Magyar, using every opportunity to emphasize its importance, both in their sermons and during informal conversations with believers. The minister at Dumbrava even adopts an extreme attitude in this matter: He forbids the use of the Romanian language in the Reformed Church and in his home, and is eager to purge the language of the local people of all Romanian words and neologisms originating in Romanian. Generally speaking, Hungarian parents send their children to Hungarian-language schools for as long as possible. It should therefore not come as a surprise that many inhabitants of homogeneous Hungarian villages such as Inucu have little or no knowledge of Romanian, which prompts much criticism from the Romanian community. Moreover, the Romanians have a negative view of Magyar. According to the Romanian villagers, Magyar is a rough, 'unsensuous' and typically barbaric language. In their opinion, the rough tonality of Magyar is in sharp contrast with the musical and poetic character they attribute to the Romanian language. It is clear that these views reflect their perception of the Hungarian people.

The Hungarians' feelings about the Romanians is manifest in the attitude they adopt towards the Romanian Orthodox religion. In general the Reformed Hungarians are very sceptical and even disdainful of the, in their eyes, exaggerated worship of saints and icons in the Romanian Orthodox Church. Some mock the numerous feast days on which Orthodox believers are not allowed to work as well as the concomitant superstition. Furthermore, the quality of the theological training of the Orthodox priests is considered to be inferior to that of their own ministers. To most ethnic Hungarians, the moral and theological superiority of their Reformed Church is beyond question.

Moreover, many Hungarians are aware that their religion still safeguards their identity, as it did during the communist era.

### 3.3. The 'right of primogeniture' to Transylvania

The conflicting interpretations of the history of the Transylvanian 'homeland' are translated into real, everyday situations in various ways.

Firstly, there is disagreement between the Romanian and Hungarian villagers about the proper name of the region that includes the villages of Dumbrava, Mànàstireni and Inucu. The ethnic Hungarians maintain that they live in *Kalotaszeg*, a specific region of historical and ethnographic significance that is known for the fact that the local Hungarian traditions have been well-preserved. According to them, the name *Kalotaszeg* originates in another name; that of *Kalota*, who was the leader of the Hungarian tribe that conquered the region around 1000 AD. The name *Kalotaszeg* is unanimously accepted by all Hungarians, including those in other countries. There is even a cultural magazine that bears this name (i.e. *Kalotaszeg. Kulturalis, közélete havilop)* and in which contributions are published on the history and traditions of the *Kalotaszeg* region. Many Hungarian villagers have a subscription to this magazine. The Romanians, on the other hand, assert that their villages belong to the region of Huedin or to the Western mountain range (*Munţii Apuseni*). To them, the term *Kalotaszeg* is merely a meaningless anachronism.

Furthermore these ethnic groups have specific views on the history of their village and church. The Hungarian community of Dumbrava is convinced that the entire population of the village was once Hungarian. They maintain that the Romanians used to live in the nearby mountain villages and did not settle in their village until the 17th and 18th centuries to work on the estates of the Hungarian boyars. That is why the Hungarians of Dumbrava regard themselves as '*bàstinasi*' (i.e. natives, autochthones), while they label the Romanian villagers as '*venituri*' (i.e. they who came). The fact that their own church building is much older than the Orthodox church of the village confirms them in their belief. The Romanians, for their part, contest this view and claim that Dumbrava has always had an ethnically mixed population.

Similar controversy surrounds the history of Mànàstireni, of which there are two quite distinct monographs: one Hungarian, the other Romanian. According to the Hungarian monograph, written by a Reformed minister of the village, the first families of the village were all Hungarian (Balint 1992: 1-2). Moreover the old Hungarian church, dating from the thirteenth century, is clear evidence in the eyes of many ethnic Hungarians that they settled here before the Romanians.

The Romanian monograph is a dissertation about the folklore of the village, adapted in 1961 by a Romanian philologist of the local community. She asserts that some 1000 years ago there were Romanians living in Mànàstireni, but that they retreated to the nearby mountains in the period of the Hungarian conquest. Still according to this theory, they later left their place of refuge and resettled in the village alongside the Hungarians (Vasaru 1961: 5-6). The view that the Romanian population fled the cruel Hungarian conquerors into the mountains is also used as an explanation for the fact that the inhabitants of the nearby mountain villages, despite harsher living conditions, are all Romanian.

The Orthodox priests play an important role in the transmission of the Romanian self-image, as is illustrated by the next example. The dissertation by the Orthodox priest of Mànàstur Românesc, a village belonging to the municipality of Mànàstireni, deals with matters concerning the local Orthodox church. In the introduction we read the following:

As I was preparing this work, I stumbled upon the most extraordinary fact, namely that the first Orthodox church of Mànàstur dates from the ninth century. This is evidence of the existence of a Romanian Orthodox community *before* the arrival of the Hungarians. It proves that the Romanians are the real rulers of Transylvania (Rus 1994: 1-2).

In Mànàstireni, where ethnic Hungarians constitute a minority of 28 % of the population, even the local doll-production is interesting from an inter-ethnic point of view. A number of Hungarian women manufacture wooden dolls dressed in traditional Hungarian attire: A colourfully embroidered apron over a long pleated skirt, a white blouse with puffed sleeves, a jewelled waistcoat and a headscarf. These dolls are sold to tourists and to foreign coreligionists with whom the minister maintains contacts. The profits go to the Reformed church community of the village. Oddly, these dolls have no features (eyes, ears, nose and mouth) nor feet. The Romanian people of the village have their own explanation for this 'mutilation': According to them, the reason that the Hungarians make the dolls without feet is to indicate that their community has been living in this place for centuries; that they belong there, and are neither willing nor able to leave. The fact that they lack facial features, on the other hand, is meant to indicate to the outside world that the ethnic Hungarians in this place have lost their true identity or are unable to express it. Still according to the Romanians, the Hungarians hope to be able to add features in the future[9]. This explanation clearly refers to the polemic regarding the right of primogeniture. Moreover, it shows that the Romanians are aware of the Hungarian community's concern for the preservation of their identity.

The Hungarian woman who designed the doll, for her part, has an explanation that is not ethnic:

"All of these dolls are women whose legs directly touch the ground. With this I want to express that all local women are independent to some extent. The fact that they don't have features doesn't mean that they have lost their personal identity, but it points to the process of homogenisation in the course of history: Women have lived here for generations and have become more uniform through time".

Among the more striking expressions of the controversial Romanian and Hungarian self-images as 'the first settlers in Transylvania' are the numerous archaeological excavations. At first glance this may appear to be an innocent scientific endeavour, but in the summer of 1994 the mere announcement that excavations would be carried out in the centre of the town of Cluj prompted an agitated and emotional response from the ethnic Hungarians. The archaeological team of the National Museum of Transylvanian History and the extreme-nationalist mayor Funar wanted to dig up the central square of Cluj -the Union Square-because there were indications that they may find remains of a Roman forum there. But this decision resulted in a heated dispute, because situated on precisely this square are the centuries-old Hungarian Roman Catholic Church of Saint Michael and the famous statue of the Hungarian king Matthias, who reigned from 1458 to 1490. The Hungarian sculptor Janos Fadrusz was commissioned to make the statue in 1896 to mark the millenary of the arrival of the Magyars in Transylvania (Shafir 1994:28). To many inhabitants of Cluj, King Matthias is the symbolic link between the Romanian and Hungarian peoples, as he, who was one quarter Romanian[10], became the most popular king the Hungarians ever had. The statue is included on UNESCO's list of internationally protected historical monuments. It was soon rumoured in Cluj and environs that the excavations would cause irreparable damage to these monuments and that the statue might even be removed altogether. This aroused a wave of protest from the ethnic Hungarians. The Magyar minority regarded the statue and the church as symbols of their historical presence in Transylvania. In June 1994 several peaceful protest rallies were organised, at which the crowd was addressed by representatives of the Hungarian party UDMR[11] and prominent personalities including the Reformed bishop László Tökés, Doina Cornea (the courageous dissident of the Ceausescu regime) and Octavian Buracu (chairman of the *'Dialog Interetnic'*-centre). Appeals and letters of protest were sent to president Iliescu as well as to the Council of Europe and UNESCO. And the planned excavations were questioned in the Hungarian parliament.

Funar, however, refused to give in. He even brought the issue to a head by announcing that soon a ceremony would be held to commemorate a Roman document dating from 124 AD, in which the town of Cluj is mentioned for the first time (Shafir 1994: 29). It was clearly his intention to rake up the age-old historical dispute about 'the right of the first settlers'. The archaeological team tried on several occasions to start excavating, but they were obstructed time after time by Hungarian militants who, responding to the chimes of their churches, would occupy the square. Policemen and soldiers had to cordon off the archaeologists from the demonstrators. Eventually the government ordered a postponement of the excavations and they sent a commission of experts to analyze the situation. The leaders of the Hungarian party demanded that the local authorities '[take] into consideration the constitutional right of the Magyars of Romania to preserve those values that express their cultural identity' (Shafir 1994: 30).

On 20 July 1994 a compromise was reached: It was agreed that only one probe would be made rather than the six that had been requested, and that this would happen at a site that would endanger neither the statue nor the church of Saint Michael.

The whole issue got a lot of media attention and the villagers followed events closely. Some Romanians believed that the Hungarians were not really concerned about the statue of king Matthias, but that they used this as an argument to prevent the excavations for fear that the Roman remains might deliver definite proof of the validity of the Romanian theory of descent and continuity.

The Hungarians, on the other hand, regarded the excavations as an attempt by Funar to minimise the Hungarian character of Transylvania and Cluj.

By october 1995 the work had not yet been completed. Some Romanians of Mànàstireni proudly asserted that archaeologists had already found a Roman oven. Hungarian villagers played down the importance of the discovery by pointing out that relics of Roman civilisation are found anywhere in Europe. Some even expressed doubts about the genuineness of the find.

In fact the central square of Cluj clearly illustrates the flaming topicality of an ancient historical controversy.

### 3.4. *The Gypsies*

As regards the Gypsies of Dumbrava and Mànàstireni, it is not so much their self-image as the sum of characteristics attributed to them by non-Gypsies that is decisive in everyday inter-ethnic relations within the village communities. Though the Gypsies of these villages are tolerated, they are not held in high esteem. Romanian and Hungarian villagers, insofar as they do not need the Gypsies, try to avoid them as much as possible. In Mànàstireni most of the Gypsies live on the edge of the village. Some villagers call the Gypsies' settlement the 'valea cotetelor' ('valley of pigsties') because it consists mainly of small dilapidated houses. But the way in which the Gypsies are perceived by the non-Gypsy community is not only reflected in where they live; it is also reflected in their cemeteries. In some villages, including Dumbrava, Bedeciu and Câpusu Mic, Gypsies are buried at a separate cemetery.

This illustrates how the other villagers and their priests regard the Gypsies' ethnicity to be more important than their religious affinity.

Gypsies possess neither land nor cattle, and, as far as their livelihood is concerned, they are now extremely dependent on their immediate social and natural environment. Certain livelihoods in the villages seem to be characteristic of this ethnic group: They are shepherds, cowherds, musicians, day labourers, they pick and sell wild fruit, and they beg. The appreciation of Gypsies as 'a group that is tolerated but not truly accepted' is also reflected in this social structure: They herd sheep and cattle but do not possess any livestock; they work the land but do not own it; they play music at parties but are not allowed to take part in the dancing.

## 4. The historical foundations of the ethnic self-images

The claim that the Romanians, Hungarians and Gypsies have only now, after the fall of Ceausescu, become ethnically conscious and concerned for the preservation of their own cultural and ethnic identity cannot be substantiated. The ethnic awakening of these communities is, in fact, the result of a long historical process. Pilon rightly points out that each people has its own specific past and that "their experiences with self-government, with enslaving or being enslaved by others, are part of their national memories. These memories then form part of a nation's 'mentality' and its members' attitudes towards themselves and others. They are as important to understand the complex nature of national self-image as are the linguistic, cultural, and territorial dimensions" (Pilon 1992: 21).

## 4.1. *Historical background*

The national awakening of Romanians and Hungarians took place in the late 18th and 19th centuries, but a true understanding of this process requires an insight into the socio-political circumstances of these peoples in the preceding centuries.

Since the end of the 9th century Transylvania had been controlled by Hungarian tribes. The Hungarian king Stephen incorporated the region into his kingdom in 1003 AD and his subjects would gradually embrace Christianity. In 1437 the *Unio Trium Nationum* (Union of the Three Nations) was founded, which implied that Transylvania would, from then on, be governed by a Diet made up of the elites of three 'nations': Magyars, Szeklers and Saxons. Each 'nation' had a number of rights and privileges and was sovereign within certain parts of Transylvania. Despite their substantial number, the Orthodox Romanians had no representation in the Diet and lived mainly as serfs and peasants lacking political rights. Romanians could only acquire a certain social status by their assimilation into the Hungarian 'nation', which involved, among other things, conversion to Catholicism or Protestantism (The Romanian Research Group 1977: 139).

In 1526 the Ottoman Empire brought about the dismemberment of the Hungarian kingdom. As a vassal state of the Ottoman Empire, Transylvania enjoyed relative independence. At the end of the 17th century, the Habsburg empire acquired Hungary and Transylvania from the Ottomans. The Habsburg Emperor, in the *Diploma Leopoldinum* of 1691, confirmed the 'union of the three nations', and their religions alone (viz. Catholicism, Calvinism, Unitarianism and Lutheranism) were recognized by law, leaving Eastern Orthodoxy, the religion of the Romanians, a merely tolerated creed (Detrez 1992: 25-26). During the implementation of their policy of centralization, the Habsburg rulers constantly had to contend with the powerful Hungarian aristocracy and their acquired constitutional rights.

According to Katherine Verdery, the attempts by Habsburg rulers to construct a strong state actually stimulated both the development of Hungarian nationalism and the awaking of the Romanian ethnic consciousness (Verdery 1983: 113-125).

4.2. *The Romanians*

The Habsburg policies were directed towards maximum integration of conquered regions and (re)catholicizing their populations. In order to accomplish these goals in Transylvania, the Habsburg government sought the support of the Orthodox Romanians. In exchange for their joining the Roman Catholic Church, the Austrians pledged to give the Orthodox clergy the same freedom and privileges as the clergy of the four recognized religions. The conversion merely involved the recognition of the pope's authority and the acceptance of four points of doctrine. Their own Orthodox customs, such as rituals, holy days, and tolerance of non-celibate priesthood, were not affected. On 5 September 1700 the union of the Orthodox and the Roman Catholic Church was accepted by an Orthodox synod at Alba Iulia (Hitchins 1983: 9-10). This marked the birth of the Greek Catholic Church, also known as the Uniate Church[12].

The most important side-effect of the formation of the Greek Catholic Church was the creation of a Romanian intellectual elite which immediately heralded the rise of Romanian nationalism. A number of Uniate priests were given an opportunity to go and study abroad; in Rome, Vienna or Paris. This education provided them with the ingredients for the Romanian national ideology: While studying Latin, philosophy and history, Romanian clergy-intellectuals became convinced of the Latin foundations of the Romanian language, and thus of the Roman ancestry of their people.

However, they were not the discoverers of their Latin origin. The idea of the Romanians' Roman descent had originally surfaced in the 14th century: Pope Clement VI mentioned in a letter written in 1345 that 'Roman Vlachs' were living in the Transylvanian region of Hungary. And this theory was further developed in the 15th and 16th centuries by such Italian humanists as Bracciolini, Aeneas Sylvius and Bonfini (Vékony 1989: 119-120). But what was new in the 18th century was that the theory about the ethnogenesis of the Romanians was used as a means of exerting political pressure in the struggle for the emancipation of the Romanian people. The concept of the 'priority' of the Romanians in Transylvania and the 'nobility' of their descent appeared for the first time as a politico-historical argument in the writings of the Greek Catholic bishop Micu Klein (1735)[13].

The role played by religious figures - initially mainly Uniate, but later also Orthodox - in the Romanian national awakening should not be underestimated. At the end of the 18th century three Greek Catholic intellectuals (viz. Clain, Sincai and Maior) wrote the first modern scholarly histories of the Romanians, in which they proved the Latin origin of the Romanian language, thereby 'demonstrating' the direct descent of the Romanian people from the Roman colonists. Hence, they regarded the Magyars, Szeklers and Saxons, who did not arrive in Transylvania until the Middle Ages, as 'newcomers' (Hitchins 1983: 30-31). But this theory soon came under attack from the Hungarians. Hungarian historians pointed to the lack of evidence for Romanian continuity, as there was nothing that could prove their presence in Transylvania during the first millennium. The Romanians were obliged to refine their thesis and developed the Daco-Roman continuity theory. Furthermore, the higher clergy wrote a number of petitions, the best-known of which is the so-called *Supplex Libellus Valachorum*, which was submitted to emperor Leopold II in 1791. They demanded that the Romanians be granted the same constitutional rights as their Magyar, Szekler and Saxon neighbours, and that the Romanian Orthodox religion be fully recognized (Pilon 1992: 49).

In fact, they wanted to restore 'ancient rights' which had been eroded during times of aristocratic hegemony, by asserting their direct descent from the Roman colonists. These efforts, however, were unsuccessful and gradually the influence of church leaders began to be challenged by an increasingly vocal class of lay intellectuals. According to Keith Hitchins, these intellectuals took a different view of history. Though they accepted the Daco-Roman continuity theory, they 'no longer based their demands for national equality primarily upon historical rights. Natural law and the concept of unalienable human rights seemed to them to be more compelling arguments' (Hitchins 1983: 52).

But the historical myths had already taken on a life of their own, spreading among the Romanian people. After the first World War, the immense Austrian-Hungarian Empire collapsed and Transylvania became a part of Greater Romania. The Transylvanian Hungarians were now a minority within the Romanian state. The myths about the history of Transylvania re-emerged with great vehemence, especially in the 1930s, with the rise of fascism in both Romania and Hungary.

The fascist elites of either country laid claim to Transylvania, using nationalistic ideology to legitimize their position (The Romanian Research Group 1977: 139). After the second World War, the historical myths were initially pushed into the background by the Russification campaign conducted by the Communist regime. But later, under the National Communism of Ceausescu, they were brought to the fore again to be elevated, as it were, into a dogma.

## 4.3. *The Magyars*

Just like the Romanian self-image, the present-day Hungarian self-image is firmly embedded in history. Their myth of descent and their Christian identity are rooted in the Middle Ages. These elements have, throughout history, been present to a varying extent, depending on the political context.

Towards the end of the 13th century, Simon Kéza included the myth of Hunor and Magor, the founders of the Huns and the Magyars, in his chronicle *Gesta Hungarorum* ('the deeds of the Hungarians'), thereby interlinking the history of these two peoples. The Hunnish leader Attila is glorified in this work as a hero and a great nomadic king. According to Szönyi, the Hungarians used this myth of origin as an ideological argument to justify their conquest of the Carpathian Basin (Szönyi 1993: 39). The myth of the Hunnish-Hungarian affinity and continuity was, in the late Middle Ages, part of the historical awareness of the Hungarian nobility and it was important in legitimizing their privileged status (Vogel 1995: 74-75). During the following centuries, this myth lingered on in the historical consciousness of the Magyars. Glatz points out that Hungarian historiography at the beginning of the 19th century returned to the theme of kinship with the courageous Huns (Glatz 1983: 32). Hungarian poets of this period also tended to look back on the glorious episodes in Hungarian history. Arany Janos' national epic about the Huns is a case in point (Cushing 1993: 66). Despite the fact that modern Hungarian historians have long since demonstrated that the common descent of these two peoples is merely a figment of the imagination of Hungarian chroniclers, lacking any historical evidence, this myth is still very much alive among rural Hungarians today.

In the course of history, the Magyars have concurrently kept alive the ideas that they are a Christian people, christianized under the reign of king Stephen (997-1038), and that they fought fiercely to safeguard Western Christianity from the influence of foreign religions. Legends about king St Stephen and about the later king St Ladislas were already told in the 11th and 12th centuries, but became particularly popular during the late Middle Ages, when the Hungarian leaders had to face Ottoman aggressors. For this purpose, Hungarian kings were depicted as archetypal Christian champions, the scourges of the pagans (Szönyi 1993: 38). But the myth relating the Magyars to Christianity was also tied to the interests of the new landed Hungarian aristocracy because it gave them the legitimizing support of a higher religion (Armstrong 1982: 51). According to Barany, the image of Hungary as the shield of Christianity is, historically speaking, based on the determined struggle of the Hungarians against the advancing Islamic Ottomans in the 15th and 16th centuries. This view on Hungary was, from as early as the 16th century, widely popularized in the Magyar vernacular (Barany 1981: 349). In addition, this author points out that, as was the case with their myth of descent, the myth about the Hungarians' Christian identity was later, especially in the 19th and early 20th centuries, used - perhaps even abused - for legitimizing expansion and the supremacy of Magyars over other nationalities of the Kingdom (Barany 1981: 349).

It is, in fact, very difficult to reconcile the pride that the Hungarians take in their descending from the pagan nomadic Huns with their emphasis on being Christians, but according to Armstrong, 'the availability of two very different myths, alternating in intensity, may well have been instrumental in preserving the unusual Magyar ethnic identity, which otherwise might have become vulnerable to recurring pressures of assimilation' (Armstrong 1982: 51).

As we have already mentioned, language is presently an important component of the Hungarian self-image. The historical origin of this linguistic consciousness lies in the era of reform towards the end of the 18th century: The attempts by Emperor Joseph II to impose German as the common language in his multilingual empire met with resistance and brought about a linguistic revival. Partly under the influence of Herder's idea that a nation lives in and through its language, Hungarians became aware of the great importance of Magyar for the preservation of their singularity (Basa 1993: 24). During the 19th century, when political nationalism was in full development, Magyar rapidly became a symbol of their national identity[14].

The Treaty of Trianon (1920) suddenly produced a situation that had been totally unforeseen: The defeat of the Austro-Hungarian empire. As Transylvania was ceded to Romania, the Hungarians who were living there were suddenly cut off from their Hungarian 'motherland'. Their status of rulers was reduced to that of an ethnic minority. Within this altered socio-political context, the Transylvanian Hungarians had to build up a new identity: a Transylvanian identity. Therefore, the ethnic Hungarians immersed themselves in their own Transylvanian history. Their historical fate, their traditions and the continuity of their presence in this region were all important in this respect. They believed, among other things, that they had a distinct Hungarian-Transylvanian tradition dating back to the 17th and 18th centuries, when the Principality of Transylvania was one of the centres of Hungarian national culture (Pomogats 1993: 102, 106). The conviction that Hungarians had been living in Transylvania for ages was used as an argument to illustrate the injustice of the Trianon Treaty.

## 4.4. *The Gypsies*

It is by no means easy to indicate particular periods in history in which the self-image of the Gypsies of Dumbrava and Mànàstireni may be rooted. The question of how the Gypsies picture themselves is closely connected with how they are perceived by the non-Gypsy community. Yet this -generally denigratory- image is undoubtedly embedded in their past.

The first groups of Gypsies probably arrived in the Romanian provinces of Walachia and Moldavia at the end of the 11th century (Crowe 1991: 61). They did not appear in Transylvania until the 14th century. Consequently, Gypsies are not involved in the polemics regarding the right of primogeniture to Transylvania.

Initially, the Gypsies in the Romanian regions were blacksmiths and craftsmen, but in the 13th century they were enslaved for various economic, military and social reasons. This slavery was institutionalized in the course of the 15th century (Crowe 1991: 62).

Beck demonstrates that the Gypsies' history of slavery lies at the origin of the ubiquitous prejudice against this people. As a result of slavery, a process in which some groups reduce others to objects, Gypsies were typified as 'universally marginal sub-humans' (Beck 1989: 54). Once this notion had been allowed to take root, it became impossible to regard Gypsies, not even the ones in important professions, in any other way. 'In reaching an understanding of prejudice against Gypsies, it is the generalized dehumanization of them as a class that became the overwhelmingly dominant perspective adopted by Romanians' (Beck 1989: 59).

Slavery was officially abolished in Romania in 1864, but for many Gypsies this did not bring about much change: Many continued to work on the estates of powerful landlords and cloisters, by which they were exploited (Crowe 1989: 67). Nevertheless, towards the end of the 19th century, a certain degree of ethnic self-consciousness had started to grow among Gypsies: In 1879 a conference took place at Kisfalu, in Hungary, to explore ways for Gypsies to acquire political and civil rights.

But a true Gypsy movement did not emerge in Romania until the 1930s, when the general economic crisis had intensified the traditional prejudiced image of Gypsies according to which they were 'untouchables' and 'indolent and lazy' (Crowe 1989: 68-69). 1930 saw the publication of the first Gypsy magazine *(Neamul Tigànesc* or 'The Gypsy People'), and three years later the General Association of Roma in Romania was founded. This was an association that openly supported nationalist ideas and which, despite surviving for only one year, launched two widely circulating magazines, viz. *Glasul Romilor* and *O Rom* (Hancock 1989: 141). In 1933 the world Gypsy congress, 'United Gypsies of Europe', was organised in Bucharest. The themes included the strengthening of feelings of ethnic solidarity among Gypsies, the commencement of the struggle against social injustice, the proclamation of 23 December as commemoration day marking the abolition of servitude, and the introduction of a national flag (two horizontal bars; the upper blue, the lower green). Just one year later, a national congress established the *Uniunea Generalà a Romilor din România* (General Union of Roma of Romania) (Crowe 1989: 69-70).

But the second World War and the persecution of Gypsies by the Nazis, also known as the *'Parajmos'*, brought this emancipatory movement to an end. After the war the Gypsies did not receive the same official recognition as the country's other 'cohabiting nationalities' because, in the eyes of the communist policymakers, they had no 'protecting state', no history, and no culture.

Not until recently, after the fall of communism, has there been a revival of the Gypsy consciousness among some Gypsy sub-communities. Certain Gypsy leaders are trying to convince the Gypsies that they all belong to the same people which migrated from India to Europe, and that they should once again unite. They regard the division of the Gypsies as a consequence of hostile external factors that must be neutralized so that unity could be restored. As a symbol of their unity, these Gypsy sub-groups adopted the anthem '*dzelem dzelem*', which had previously been chosen as the Gypsy anthem at a Romany world congress near London in 1971 (Hancock 1989: 145). Moreover the Gypsies in Romania have established a number of political parties that now have some parliamentary representatives to protect their rights. Some argue in favour of education in the Gypsy language (i.e. Romany) to solve the problem of illiteracy among Gypsies and to prevent that children would lose their native tongue. The demands formulated by the Gypsy groups that stand up for their identity seem to be inspired by a cultural nationalism without territorial implications. Others strive towards a complete integration in Romanian society. Discord among the numerous Gypsy groups appears to be one of the most important obstacles to truly accomplishing something for their people.

But this emancipatory movement has only gained a foothold in a certain section of the Gypsy population. As yet, this does not include the Gypsies of Dumbrava and Mànàstireni.


## 5. Conclusion

Transylvania, the mountainous motherland, lends its inhabitants a specific communality that transcends the secularizing, categorizing language differences. Nevertheless, five centuries of Hungarian dominance from the beginning of the second millennium, followed by an Ottoman era of two centuries, and particularly the subsequent centuries of Habsburg rule, have resulted in persistent relations and mutual perceptions between Magyars and Romanians, as well as the image of Magyars and Romanians respectively as protectors of the border of the Occident and of Christianity against advancing Islam, which is concurrently labelled as anti-Western.

This has led to a matrix, based on ethno-religious elements, in which 'we' is juxtaposed with 'the other', while at the bottom of this common frame of reference, the Gypsies are tolerated as a non-identity: Transylvania, a singularity within the Romanian nation.

*Notes*

1.  The term 'Romanians' does, in fact, have two meanings: (i) the citizens of the country; (ii) the native speakers of the Romanian language or the 'ethnic Romanians'. When I use the term 'Romanians', it is in the second sense.

2.  The terms 'ethnic Hungarians' and 'Hungarians' are used interchangeably to refer to Romanian citizens of Hungarian origin. The ethnic Hungarians refer to themselves as 'Magyars'

3.  Despite the fact that most Romanian historians deny the mythical character of this theory and try to prove its scientific nature by means of historical evidence, we can justifiably speak of a 'myth'. Firstly, because its historical accuracy is questioned by other historians. Secondly because this doctrine actually functions as a myth: It provides the Romanian people with a worthy collective identity and enhances their solidarity as a group.

4.  This theory too is adhered to by most Romanian historians.

5.  See, among others, the official Hungarian textbook for the third school grade: Magyar nyelv. Tankönyv a III. osztaly szamara, Bucuresti: Editura didactică si pedagogică 1992: 45-46.

6.  There are several versions of this myth. See, for example, Wass 1979: 12-16; Szönyi 1993: 56.

7.  The anthem also alludes to other elements of the Romanian self-image, including their struggle against the barbarians, their Christian identity and the conviction that their land has always been Romanian.

8.  Here are two examples: The word *pîine* (bread) has been replaced with *pâine*, which indicates very clearly that it is etymologically derived from the Latin word *panis*; and the conjugation *sînt* (I am) has been replaced with *sunt*, which resembles the Latin form *sum*.

9.  Presently, dolls are also produced with features, to meet demand from foreigners who prefer dolls with a face. So now people have a choice between dolls with and without features. However, all dolls still lack feet.

10. Many Romanians even regard king Matthias, whom they refer to as Matei Corvin, as half Romanian and half Hungarian. His father is said to have been a Romanian nobleman. They call him *Iancu din Hunedoara*, while the Hungarians speak of *Janos Hunyadi*.

11. UDMR is the abbreviation of *Uniunia Democraticà Maghiarà din România* or Hungarian Democratic Federation of Romania.

12. See Wesselink 1992 for more information about the Greek Catholic Church in Transylvania.

13. For the most important recent assessment of Micu's role as a national leader, see David Prodan 1971: 134-94.

14. In 1833 the official language of Hungary was changed from Latin to Magyar (Pilon 1992: 43).

# Chapter VI:

## 'Biological' Christianity and Ethnicity: Spain's Construct from Past Centuries

Christiane Stallaert

### 1. The Spaniard and his opposite, the Moor

Américo Castro (1983: 13; 1987: 197) describes the genesis of the Spanish as an ethnic group as a reaction to contacts with the Moors. The Basques, the Catalans, the Asturians etc. started to define themselves as 'Christians' in their struggle with the Muslims, so that religion was able to become the principal ethnic emblem of these future 'Spaniards'.

If one subscribes to this theory, one accepts that the ethnic identification of the Spaniard with Christianity is an 'accident' of history; a process that can be reconstructed by means of historical material. This Christian identity is, in other words, not regarded as an 'essential' characteristic of the Spaniard, but as one that was acquired in the course of the Reconquista. It is clear that this insight violates the traditional ethnic belief of the Spaniard. It questions the very essence of his ethnic identity.

The essentialist theories about the Spanish Christian identity are central to Spanish ethno-nationalist doctrine. Manuel García Morente, with his book *Ideas para una filosofía de la Historia de España* published in 1943, is representative of Spanish ethno-nationalist thought. According to this author, Catholicism is 'consubstantial' with the Spaniard, while the ethnic opposite of the Spaniard is undoubtedly the 'Moor' (García Morente 1943: 66 ff.). Thomas F. Glick (1991: 12) points out that the present-day Spaniard still regards the Moor as the Other par excellence, the 'quintessence of the foreigner, an object of fear', and he refers to recent Spanish research in the field of clinical psychology to support this theory. Clinical psychology aside, there are abundant examples in contemporary Spain illustrating the association of the 'Moor' with the 'Other'.

In Reconquest Spain, the expression '*moros y cristianos*' meant 'everyone' (Castro 1987: 51-52). Today, the Spaniard still symbolically divides humanity into two categories: Christians and Moors[1]. The expression '*o todos moros o todos cristianos*', for example, means that all people are equal before the law. Anything that complies with the own ethnic norm is called Christian; everything else is 'Moorish'. The imagery of Christians versus Moors is very noticeable in the socialization process. A child must learn 'who are the Moors and who the Christians'. It is taught to behave like a 'Christian', though this notion has nothing to do with religion[2]. The Christian institution of marriage is contrasted with concubinage, which is referred to as '*juntarse como los moros*'.

The preceding characterization of Spanish ethnicity allows us to situate the ethnogenesis of the Spaniards in time. Ethnically speaking, it only makes sense to refer to the inhabitants of the Iberian peninsula as Spaniards after their coming into contact with the 'Moor', that is to say after AD 711. It is just as nonsensical to refer to the Hispano-Visigothic population, the Hispano-Roman population or the Iberians as 'Spaniards' as it is to refer to the Romans as 'Italians'. The thesis of A. Castro that all events on the Iberian peninsula dating from before the period of the Islamic occupation and the Reconquista can not be referred to as 'Spanish' is confirmed in the historical consciousness of the average present-day Spaniard. Artefacts and customs that are believed to have originated in a distant past or a foreign culture are attributed to Moorish times. In everyday language, the expression '*tiempo de los moros*' is often used as a repository; a conglomerate of objects and facts which the Spaniard situates in a kind of 'ethnic prehistory'. The Roman and Visigothic eras, on the other hand, do not appear to be relevant to the historical consciousness of the present-day Spaniard. Though often dating from the pre-Islamic age, many monuments and techniques are, by oral tradition, placed historically in "Moorish times". Examples of this association are the cave dwellings cut into the tufa in the region of Guadix (Granada), the typical villages of the Alpujarra, and certain irrigation techniques used in agriculture[3]. Menéndez Pelayo (*Heterodoxos*, part I, book I, p. 214) describes how certain neolithic burial grounds on the Baleares are referred to in the vernacular as '*cementerios de moros*'.

And an inhabitant of Talamanca de Jarama near Madrid actually told me that the local Roman bridge was built by the Moors!

The reference to Moorish times has also remained a fixed ingredient of Spanish folklore and legends. The founding legends of quite a few Spanish villages go back to the Moorish era, which in some cases is confused with a mythic biblical past[4]. The consecutive confrontations with the Moor in the course of Spanish history have converged in the historical memory of the Spaniard and are usually placed in the 8th century AD. During the Civil War (1936-1939), the occupation of the territory by Franco's troops was described as a Moorish occupation, *'cuando los moros tomaron la ciudad'*. In the stories told in the Spanish country about the Moorish presence during the civil war (and, in the region of Asturias, about their presence during the suppression of the miners' strikes in 1934), this more recent contact with the Moor has merged with the historical Islamic era after AD 711[5].

The correlation between Christianity and not being a Moor in the Spanish ethnic identity finds expression in the concept of *'casticismo'*[6], which may be defined as the ethnic (viz. the biological-genealogical) identification of the Spaniard with Christianity, conceived as the opposite of Islam. The outstanding symbol of *casticismo* is Santiago Matamoros, the 'Slayer of Moors', patron saint of Spain.

*Casticismo* has earned Spain a unique character within the Christian world[7]. Though in other Christian countries Islam is equally regarded as the negation of the own religious identity, the Muslim is not necessarily perceived there as a threat to the ethnic purity. Nor is Christianity regarded as the essence of the ethnic identity[8]. But in the eyes of the Spanish this is the case. According to Spanish ethnicity, the preservation of Christian purity demands a defensive attitude towards any possible 'Moorish'/'Jewish' taint.

The specificity of Spanish Christianity is apparent in the numerous periods of tension through the ages between the Spanish state and the Vatican. More often than not this tension was connected with the values of *casticismo*. With the setting up of the Inquisition, the Spanish state and Church came into conflict with the Pope, who regarded the distinction between Old and New Christians to be contrary to Christian doctrine[9]. The Popes also took a negative view of the purity statutes which would dominate Spanish society from the 16th century onwards[10]. As regards the ordination of mestizos and mulattos in the New World, there was a difference of opinion up until the 18th century between the Spanish Crown and the Vatican. While the Vatican regarded baptism to be a sufficient criterion for access to priesthood, the Spanish colonizer adhered to an ethnic criterion based on Old Christian ancestry[11]. The expulsion measure of 1609 applying to the Moriscos did not have the Pope's seal of approval, despite the pressure that was exerted on him by the Spanish lobby in Rome[12]. The measure taken in 1609 was, by the way, unique in the history of Christendom, as it concerned the expulsion of a group of Christians from Christian territory. The Spanish, on the other hand, often took umbrage at the lack of interest on the part of the Vatican for ethno-religious purity. It was, for example, incomprehensible to sixteenth and seventeenth-century Spain that the Pope tolerated Jewish converts and their descendants in his entourage[13].

It is Américo Castro who drew attention to the importance of *casticismo* to Spanish history and culture. The conflict of the castes may be regarded as a point of departure for the study of the Spanish ethnogenesis[14]. The different phases of this ethnogenesis roughly correspond with the three major periods into which Américo Castro (1972: 30) subdivides Spanish history: The period of *convivencia* of the three castes (up until the late 14th century); the disruption of this social order as a result of the *converso*-issue and the search for a new equilibrium (up until the 17th century); the hegemony of the Old Christian caste (from the 17th century to the present).

## 2. The Spanish ethnogenesis

### 2.1. *Convivencia: Christians, Moors and Jews*

In Spanish historiography, the term *convivencia* refers to the specific social system that allowed a more or less harmonious coexistence of three ethno-religious communities on the Iberian peninsula and which lasted from the Reconquista until the era of the Catholic Kings. The significance of this period to the formation of Spanish ethnicity is now universally acknowledged.

The collective consciousness of Christian Spain, in which the religious identity became the central point, developed during the eight centuries of the Reconquista. After the reconquest of the territory from the Moors, the process of repopulation of recovered ground was not an entirely Christian affair. Demographic circumstances did not allow the use of strict selection criteria, and the Christian reconquerors also had to call upon the ethnic-religious minorities, viz. Jews and Moors, to safeguard the demographic (and the economic) continuity of recaptured regions[15].

The society which was thus created was based on the coexistence of three religious 'castes', whereby the Christians enjoyed an absolute monopoly of power. The epitaph on the grave of Ferdinand III, the reconqueror of Seville, is symbolic of this social structure. The inscription consists of a text in Latin, Castilian, Arabic and Hebrew (Castro 1971:38-39). While the Latin text indicates that the Christians were the dominant caste, the use of the three other languages clearly illustrates that Ferdinand III ruled over a multi-ethnic society based on a triple segmentation into religious castes (Cardaillac 1991: 15-16).

The position of the individual in this *convivencia* society was determined by birth. From birth, each individual belonged to the Christian, the Jewish or the Moorish caste. Each religious caste was a closed community: Passing from one caste to another was practically impossible. The separateness and purity of each caste were safeguarded by a number of social mechanisms such as the condemnation of apostasy, proselytism and exogamy[16]. The naming of children had to conform with the norm of the caste. The Christian leaders guarded the religious orthodoxy of each caste and tried to ensure through legislation that the Moorish and the Jewish communities would comply with Islamic and Jewish religious rules. The ethno-religious purity was measured by means of a biological criterion, sc. the extent to which the caste, and each lineage within the caste, had been preserved from mixing with members of other castes. The ethnic ideal of purity of the blood (*limpieza/pureza de sangre*) was the best guarantee for the preservation of caste endogamy. As a result, the *conversos* (converts from other castes) were also forced into endogamy, so that it could be said that they in turn formed a caste within society. In relation to the Jewish, Moorish and Christian castes, the *converso*-castes were regarded as 'impure'.

Contact between the communities was governed by strict rules of segregation that were intended to protect the religious purity of the castes. These laws included bans on cohabitation, the nourishing and nurturing of children belonging to another caste, eating food or taking medicine which had been sold or prepared by members of another caste, participating in one another's social life etc. Apart from the strictly regulated segregation system, there were principles at work to guarantee mutual tolerance between the castes. The policies of the authorities took into account the fundamental characteristics of each caste. Jews, for example, were allowed to observe their Sabbath, to have synagogues, and to possess religious books. Furthermore, the Christian lawmakers safeguarded the sacrosanctity of the synagogue and, in 'mixed' lawsuits, would refrain from imposing obligations that went against Jewish or Islamic law.

### 2.2. *'o todos moros o todos cristianos'*

After a gradual erosion of this social model in the course of the 15th century, the fate of *convivencia* was officially sealed in 1492. The contrast between the quadrilingual epitaph on the grave of the Holy Ferdinand and the Latin one on that of Ferdinand and Isabella undeniably reflects the fact that the history of Spanish ethnicity was entering a new era. With their anti-Moorish and anti-Jewish policy, Ferdinand and Isabella responded to the urgent need for a solution to the *converso*-issue, which had arisen at the end of the 14th century and had caused a disruption of the caste system.

The term *converso* (convert) is a general term applying to the Morisco, -*mudéjar* or Muslim under Christian rule who has converted to Christianity-, as well as the *marrano*, also known as *judeoconverso* or *confeso*, a Jewish convert to Christianity.

While the term 'convert' may be associated with the notion of religious conviction, it should be pointed out that in most cases the conversion was limited to baptism, which usually happened *en mass* and under duress.

The Jewish *converso*-issue had arisen towards the end of the 14th century when, during a wave of anti-Semitism prompted by social and economic problems, a great many Jews resigned themselves to mass baptism. The mass conversions of Muslims happened later, around the beginning of the 16th century. In the region of Valencia, these conversions were linked with the *germanías*, a social protest aimed at breaking the power of the local aristocracy. Whereas in Andalusia, they were the result of the tough integration policy pursued by Cardinal Cisneros.

With the creation of great masses of *conversos*, the triple pattern of the social system, based on 'pure' castes (Moors, Jews and Christians by birth), was eroded and the Christian caste was subdivided into two categories. On the one hand, there were the *cristianos viejos*, the Old Christians and consequently *castizos* (of pure descent) or *lindos* (derived from *legítimos*, which means 'authentic' or 'of pure race'); and on the other, the *cristianos nuevos* (New Christians) or *conversos*, who were not of Christian origin.

The segregation principle, which was a precondition for the *convivencia*, had been completely undermined, and Spanish society would have to search for a new equilibrium. With the *conversos*, the Christian caste was suddenly confronted with members who were not ethnic Christians and did not in the least behave like Christians in the sociocultural sense. The only distinction between *conversos* and Jews or Moors was baptism. The Christian authorities came to realize that proper assimilation measures with regard to these *conversos* were urgently required. They outlined a policy based on catechism and evangelism, coupled with other measures like spatial segregation of *conversos* and members of their former castes, viz. Jews and Moors. The failure of this policy resulted in the Edict of 1492, whereby all non-converted Jews were expelled from the country. The text of the Edict clearly shows that this drastic measure was connected with the assimilation policy regarding the *converso*-minority. A few years later (between 1501 and 1525), the Muslims were also banished.

## 2.3. *Purity of blood (limpieza de sangre)*

After the expulsion of *judíos* and *mudéjares* the population of Spain consisted entirely of Christians. In this new social structure, ethnic purity was the privilege of the Old Christians. They alone were *castizos*. They descended from pure Christian ancestors. The *cristianos nuevos* were labelled as *maculados* (impure, 'tainted' Christians) because of their Moorish or Jewish ancestry. They were referred to as '*cristianos nuevos de casta/generación de moros*' or '*de casta/generación de judíos*'. As a result of the pulling down of caste-boundaries and the infiltration of the Christian caste by *conversos*, two institutions were set up to tighten controls on the purity of the Christian caste and to consolidate the position of power held by the Old Christians. These institutions are the Inquisition and the purity or *limpieza*-statutes. Originating in a concern for the preservation of Old Christian ethnic purity, both institutions would in turn cause this concern to become a real obsession and perpetuate it.

The Tribunal of the Inquisition was established in November 1478 and first started operating in Seville in 1480. The immediate reason for the setting up of this tribunal was the concern about the potentially negative influence of the *conversos* on the purity of the Old Christians. It appears from an anonymous document dating from the first half of the 16th century that contemporaries too linked the setting up of the Inquisition with the disruption of the caste system: 'The three Laws, Moors, Jews and Christians had mixed considerably and the ones converted the others and the others converted the third, and it seemed as if people were furtively making a nonsense of the Laws, because in the morning they were Christians, in the afternoon they were Moors and in the evening they were Jews; and in view of these crying abuses it was warranted to expel Moors and Jews from Spain and to tear down the synagogues and mosques and to establish the Holy Inquisition with the greatest rigour' (*Memorial*, AHN, Inq., leg. 1325, ff. 13v.-14, quoted in Avilés Fernández, 1980: 186). It is striking how the geographic implementation of this institution happened according to the proportion of *conversos* in the total population (Bennassar 1984: 47).

From a social point of view, a condemnation by the Inquisition put an ineradicable stain on the purity of blood or *limpieza de sangre* of a lineage. The memory of the conviction was kept alive by the *sambenitos*. These tunics, which convicts were made to wear for a certain period, were later hung up in their local church, to remind people of the *mácula* of certain families (Bennassar 1984: 117; Kamen 1985).

A second element on which the institutionalization of the preconception of *limpieza de sangre* was based were the purity-statutes. These statutes governed access to important social institutions and positions, which meant that one had to be able to prove that one's origins were pure, that there was no Moorish or Jewish blood running through one's veins, and that one had never been confronted by the Inquisition. The introduction of *limpieza*-statutes by all kinds of institutions had a snowballing effect. As an increasing number of institutions required new members to provide proof of *limpieza*, thereby enhancing their immaculate reputation, institutions that did not set this condition of entry were inevitably suspected of impurity or *converso* sympathies. If these institutions wished to protect their reputation, they could not but give in to the obsession with *limpieza*. By the second half of the 16th century, the *limpieza*-statutes had become a general requirement for access to public, military or ecclesiastical office[17].

At first, the *limpieza*-statute was officially limited to two generations and one was required to prove that one's four grandparents were Old Christians. In practice, the obsession with *limpieza* led to the implementation of an absolute *limpieza*-criterion: It required just one distant ancestor to be impure to deprive an entire lineage of the status of Old Christian. The obsession with *limpieza* assumed such enormous social importance that, in the age of Philip II, a plan was conceived to restrict the enquiry into *limpieza* to a period of a hundred years (Domínguez Ortiz 1988: 89; Kamen 1985: 127; Sicroff 1960: 188). The suggestion got little support and was rejected.

Impurity of blood was believed to be a hereditary trait that would not be erased in the course of generations: Ethno-religious impurity was inevitably passed on from parents to a child via the umbilical cord or the mother's milk. Ideological impurities or behaviour that deviated from the Old Christian norm were also inevitably passed on through the blood. This biological determinism made it impossible for *conversos* ever to become 'good' Christians.

As the trait of being a *cristiano nuevo* was regarded as a dominant hereditary factor, the number of *cristianos nuevos* increased continuously, at the expense of the *cristianos viejos*[18]. The contamination of society by *conversos* was spreading all the time and the obsessive concern for the purity of the Old Christian caste had an adverse effect on the international reputation of the Spanish people: In the rest of the Christian world, the term *marrano* (i.e. *judeoconverso*) actually became synonymous with 'Spaniard'[19].

Also, the quality of *cristiano viejo* was under constant threat. With each new postulation or application for promotion within an institution or office, one was subjected to another *limpieza* inquiry, implying a risk that some evidence of impurity may as yet be found. Such investigations were repeated time and again for one and the same person[20]. The attempt at reform by Philip II with regard to limiting the period of time that an enquiry into *limpieza* should cover (Caro Baroja 1978 b, II: 333; Asensio 1976: 170) was repeated in 1623 during the reign of Philip IV with regard to the number of *limpieza* inquiries to which one and the same person could be subjected: It was argued that three favourable investigations should suffice to acquire the permanent status of *cristiano viejo* (Domínguez Ortiz 1988: 64 and 90; Sicroff 1960: 216; Lea 1983, II: 175). The need for reform of the *limpieza*-statute was suggested by the Inquisitor-General himself, who warned of the destructive influence of the system on the caste of the *cristianos viejos* and its paralysing effect on the functioning of society[21]. However, such reforms found no response, as the obsession with *limpieza* was already too deeply ingrained.

The biological mixing of blood with Moorish or Jewish elements through marriage with a *converso* was not the only form of contamination. Too close a contact with impure Christians was sufficient to tarnish the honour and purity of a *cristiano viejo*[22]. As was the case during the era of *convivencia*, the segregation rules were regarded as a safeguard for the purity of the caste. It was believed that the upbringing of Old Christian children, for example, should not be entrusted to *conversos*[23].

The danger of losing one's own *limpieza* through contact with impure Christians was further enhanced by the weight that was attached to one's reputation in the *limpieza* investigation. The testimony of three or four persons to someone being descended from *cristianos nuevos* was sufficient to deprive this person and all his relatives and descendants of their *honra* or honour (Domínguez Ortiz 1988: 90-91). False testimonies were encouraged by the fact that the identity of witnesses was kept secret (Revah 1971: 266-267).

Self-evidently, this verification procedure was well-exploited for giving vent to feelings of rivalry, hate or jealousy by casting a slur on the honour of a foe or a rival in the race for an office or social promotion (Chauchadis 1984: 180). The social mobility and recognition of individuals were virtually entirely controlled by their environment (Kamen 1985: 121). The power of reputation was so important in determining *limpieza* that the vaguest rumour about a possible *mácula* was a sufficient ground to officially lose one's purity. For the same reason, any contact with the Inquisition was compromising to one's *limpieza de sangre*, even if one was acquitted.

One way of safeguarding one's reputation was to condemn oneself to social immobility. If no inquiries into ancestry needed to be carried out, a certain *mácula* (taint, stain) on the lineage might fade in the collective memory as time passed. Some would therefore opt not to apply for office or promotion to a religious order and not to pretend to the hand of a *cristiana vieja* (Domínguez Ortiz 1988: 193; Caro Baroja 1978 a: 494). This social immobility was sometimes coupled with a biological immobility. The reluctance of *conversos* to bring children with a tainted lineage into the world could inspire them to celibacy (Domínguez Ortiz 1988: 192-193).

Changing a family name -the typical *converso* names were universally known and had been listed; their presence in the collective memory ensured by the *sambenitos*, the *Libros Verdes* and oral tradition (Domínguez Ortiz 1988: 191; Caro Baroja 1978 b, II: 312)- or moving to another region could complicate inquiries into ancestry (Domínguez Ortiz 1988: 199). The laborious reconstruction of the lives of certain important figures in Spanish history is seen as an indication of their 'impure' origin.

Finally, one could also resort to bribing witnesses (Chauchadis 1984: 134) or forging a genealogy to conceal a tainted lineage. As a result of the enormous social pressure on people's *limpieza*, forgery of genealogies had become a good livelihood. Noble families could 'redeem' their purity from genealogists, who in the 17th century became a national plague.

Ancestry and reputation were not the only elements to be used as evidence. A whole range of other criteria were also taken into account. The mere fact that an applicant had not been appointed to a post was reason to suspect this person of infamy (Kamen 1985: 122). The actual profession of an individual was also believed to be significant, as a distinction was made between *oficios limpios* (pure professions) and impure or *converso* professions. The importance that was attached to this occupational criterion would vary according to one's region of origin. People from a 'pure' region could much more readily devote themselves to an 'impure' or suspect professional activity (Aranzadi 1981: 355). This explains why the Basques were able to go into commerce, while for someone from an impure region this would have counted as sufficient proof of a *converso* origin (Domínguez Ortiz 1988: 208). It speaks for itself that Andalusia was regarded as the most impure region of all.

In much the same way as access to social institutions was governed by the statutes of *limpieza*, the 'pure' regions tried to protect themselves against *converso* infestation. Guipúzcoa already closed its borders to *conversos* at the end of the 15th century. In 1511 all *converso* immigrants were expelled from the territory of Vizcaya. Guipúzcoa and Vizcaya guarded their *limpieza* so vehemently that every new inhabitant was subjected to a thorough inquiry into purity of blood (Domínguez Ortiz 1988: 198). As a result of their scrupulous policy on *limpieza*, these regions had no need for a tribunal to watch over the orthodoxy of the population, and the activities of the Inquisition were rather limited there (Caro Baroja 1986, I: 360). The term *vizcaíno* became synonymous with *cristiano viejo* (Sicroff 1960: 277) and, quite ironically, even the *judeoconversos* began to call themselves *vizcaínos*, not only to represent themselves as Old Christians, but to emphasize their 'pure' descent from Abraham[24].

Villages and towns across Spain also protected their reputation of purity, as is evident from the *'Relaciones topográficas'* (Chauchadis 1984: 185). The purity of the village community was compared with that of the surrounding villages or towns. There are many examples in Spain of local sayings in which the village boundary is equated with the boundary of *limpieza* and the inhabitants of a neighbouring village are labelled as more Jewish or Moorish, and therefore less pure (Domínguez Ortiz 1988: 197-198; Caro Baroja 1978 b, III: 236-237 and 1990: 301-303).

The ideal of the recreation of Old Christian society was projected on the then recently discovered, still immaculate New World. While the restoration of purity in Spain itself had long become a lost cause, efforts were made to realize this ideal in the newly acquired overseas territories. Permission to travel to these places was, for instance, dependent on the condition of *limpieza* and was reserved for *cristianos viejos*. As a matter of fact, this policy had been suggested by Columbus himself, as is evident from his correspondence with the Catholic Kings (Todorov 1982: 48-49). Among a great many *conversos* who were thus forced to abandon their dream of emigrating was Cervantes (Castro 1974: 34).

Finally, it should be mentioned that, in the eyes of the Spaniard, a Visigothic origin was the outstanding proof of Old Christian purity. The tendency to make one's lineage trace to Visigothic ancestors originated in the 14th century and reached its peak in the 16th, at the height of the ideal of Old Christian purity (Caro Baroja 1986, I and 1978 a). The exaltation of a Gothic ideal symbolizes the pursuit of a return to untainted pre-Islamic Spain. This ideal permeated all ranks of society and it even reached the American continent (see Lipschutz, 1975).

## 3. *Casticismo* in contemporary Spain

Américo Castro (1974: 74) regards *limpieza de sangre* as the 'backbone of the Spanish soul since the 16th century'. J. Caro Baroja (1986, I: 134) notes that the statutes of *limpieza* dominated social life in Spain from the 15th to the 19th century. This author argues that to dismiss the matter as a detail is to falsify the social history of the country, as it would be to ignore the caste system in a study of India (Caro Baroja 1978 b, II: 311). While A. Domínguez, in his work *Instituciones y sociedad en la España de los Austrias*, refers to the purity of blood as *'aquel fenómeno fundamental de nuestra historia'* (1985: 26), he does qualify that point of view to a certain extent in later writings. Nevertheless, this historian too continues to recognize that a proper interpretation of the Spanish past requires an insight into the aspect of *limpieza de sangre* (Domínguez Ortiz 1986: 29 and 1991: 250).

The obsession with purity of blood as the essence of *casticismo* gives expression to the specific nature of Spanish Christian religiosity as an ethnic emblem and consequently to the originality of the Spanish ethnic identity compared to that of other Christian countries[25]. This biological Christianity, conceived as a negation of Islam, is an important key to the issue of ethnicity in Spain, not only from a historical point of view, but from a contemporary perspective as well.

The institutional pillars of *casticismo* (Inquisition and Statutes of Purity) were only gradually dismantled in the course of the 19th century; a process incidentally which involved political tension and civil war. As *casticismo* was, for many centuries, the ideological basis for Spanish nationalism and the official institutions, it should not come as a surprise that those very values (viz. biological Christianity coupled with a negation of all that is Semitic, especially Islam) are to this day a part of the ethnic identity of the Spaniard. One could even assert that, as far as their ethnic dimension is concerned, the historical developments in 20th century Spain can only be understood if one takes account of the identification framework of *casticismo*. Examples that spring to mind are the civil war (1936-1939), the rise of peripheral nationalisms and regionalisms, and the transition of a unified Spanish state into a federal structure[26].

The civil war was proclaimed a *Cruzada* by the Spanish Church; a crusade for religion, in which the Spaniard had to defend his Christian essence against the anti-Spaniard (Payne 1984: 218-220). The symbol of the anti-Spain was the second Republic with its attack on the Catholic fundamentalist regime. Azaña's enunciation during the second Republic that Spain was no longer catholic

('*España ha dejado de ser católica*') should, in the first place, be understood as a reference to the downfall of 'institutionalized casticism'. It is beyond question that an overwhelming majority of Spaniards continued to identify ethnically with Christianity as anti-Islam. Though republican Spain was portrayed by the 'national' front as the godless anti-Spain, there is sufficient evidence that *casticismo* values were also essential to the identity of a great many 'reds'. The fear of a 'Moorish' taint remained a strong cohesive factor between Spaniards during the civil war, despite the ideological discord. Fraser (1979: 275) recounts the experiences during the civil war of a right-wing judge from Seville, who was accidentally taken prisoner by the rebels and would later be freed after an intervention by Queipo de Llano:

> He was told he could spend the night in a room where a fire was burning. He pulled up a chair, but soon some Moorish troops came in. He had never liked the Moors and asked to be taken to a cell. As the warder opened the cell door he saw that there were some twenty men crammed into a tiny space trying to sleep on the floor. The prisoners began to protest. 'I said I understood but that I didn't want to spend the night in the same room with Moors. As soon as they heard the word Moors they leapt up, exclaiming. They were right'.

We learn from testimonies from Extremadura that, regardless of their ideological allegiance in the conflict, many people fled on the arrival of Franco's troops for the '*moro Juan*'. This legendary bogeyman, who during the civil war once again became a cold reality for the Spanish, inspired great fear, especially in females, 'because it was said that Juan the Moor dishonoured women'.

In his fieldwork on a Castilian village during the 1960s, Michael Kenny (1969:46) underlines the strong identification with Christianity as a common feature of all the villagers:

> Even the most cynical of men will insist that his religion (although he may not practise it) is an integral part of his existence, so that an attack on his religion is also an attack on his way of life and vice versa. Confusion arises from identifying the two at a level where we should make some distinction. Hence, anti-clericalism should be distinguished from anti-catholicism.

A little further in the same work we find a clear example of how in the eyes of 'red' Spain, too, there remained a connection between the Christian identity and a negation of being a Muslim or a Jew:

> ...even if a couple could tranquilly live together without having been married in church they would not wish their own shame (in the eyes of the people) on to their children. In the same way, the main anxiety of every mother is to have her child 'named' as soon as possible after birth, for (...) no mother in her right mind would run the risk of having her offspring called a Moor or a Jew (Kenny 1969:74).

Especially during the second Republic, many Spaniards found it difficult to reconcile their political persuasions with their ethno-religious identity. Carmelo Lisón Tolosana (1983: 292) describes how this dilemma manifested itself in the town of Belmonte de los Caballeros, in Aragon. He points out that 'in certain situations, religion came to the surface even in the most extremist republican families'. We have obtained similar testimonies for this period regarding the region of Badajoz, where children would be baptized against the wish and without the knowledge of their fathers because the mothers would not tolerate a 'Moor' in the family.

It is noticeable in present-day situations too that, when the Spaniard comes face to face with the Moor, the identification framework of *casticismo* is activated. Interesting places for studying this mechanism are Ceuta and Melilla, two Spanish enclaves in Morocco[27]. Both towns have a heterogenious population, divided into ethno-religious communities. The Christians are in the majority, followed by the Muslims, Jews and Hindus. Ceuta was conquered from the Moors by Portugal in 1415, while Melilla was taken in 1497 by the Spanish duke of Medina Sidonia. Ceuta has been Spanish territory since 1580. Because of their geographical location on the extremity of the Christian-Islamic border, these two towns are the ideal breeding ground for Spanish ethnic nationalism. The historical catalyst of the Spanish ethnogenesis is permanently present in Ceuta and Melilla. An aspects of this is the constant awareness of the Reconquista. The Christian inhabitants of Ceuta see themselves as the defenders of the Christian-Moorish border who must protect Spain against a possible new Moorish invasion. They point out that the nostalgia for al-Andalus is still very much alive amongst Muslims.

Despite a strong Muslim presence, the Christian identity emerges as the 'official' identity of both towns, and this is reflected in their streets. In Ceuta, one finds no Islamic street names and hardly any Arabic signs. While the Muslims ascribe the purely Christian appearance of the streets to a deliberate policy of ethnic cleansing, the Christians claim that it is the logical consequence of the 'pure' past of the town. After the Reconquista, Ceuta was cleansed of all Muslim elements, and the current Muslim presence is - or so the Christians assert - a recent phenomenon resulting from predominantly illegal immigration from Morocco. In some instances the mythologization of the ethnic purity of Ceuta has led to a complete denial of the Islamic episode in the history of this town. In August 1989, a government representative in Ceuta told us that:

> "...Ceuta has never experienced any Arab influence at all. Ceuta used to be a passageway for Arabs on their way to Europe, but Arabs never settled there. The Islamic population of Ceuta dates from after the civil war. There has never been any Arab feeling here. Never. This town does not have an Arab past; Ceuta has never been Arabic or Islamic or Moroccan. Never. Ceuta has always been something else. The Portuguese or the Phoenician influence is more noticeable than the Islamic. And that is logical, because the Arab has never been here. That is why one can only smile when Morocco claims this town" (personal statement).

The Muslims, for their part, claim that some Islamic families have been living in Ceuta for four centuries. According to them, the present-day Spaniard descends from the former Moorish occupier. With this viewpoint they deny the Spanish ideal of *limpieza* and the Old Christian interpretation of the nation's past. Moreover, they accuse the Christians of historical parochialism. If one pursues the historical analysis further, one cannot but concede - according to this thesis - that Ceuta was a Moorish town before the Christian presence. On the basis of this reasoning, the organization of Terra Omnium in Melilla claims that the Christians are the real immigrants, while the indigenous inhabitant of the territory is the 'Moor' - the Berber to be precise. In November 1986 the Islamic Collective, under the leadership of Aomar Mohamedi Dudú, proclaimed a reversal of the ethnic balance of power in the following statement: 'The Islamic Collective of Melilla pronounces the Arabic and Islamic character of the town of Melilla and raises no objections to the integration of any other collective in its

Arabic and Islamic social fabric' (El Faro de Ceuta, 9 Nov. 1986). In an interview broadcast on Spanish television, Dudú repeated his proposition and he called Melilla an 'Arabic, Islamic and Maghrebi town'. The Spanish presence was challenged as illegitimate. Against the Muslim claim of greater seniority, the Christians set the myth of their Visigothic origins and they draw attention to the fact that, when the Muslims invaded Ceuta and Melilla in the 8th century AD, these towns were under Visigothic rule.

They argue that it would therefore be appropriate for the town authorities to promote the Visigothic heritage, in tourist brochures for example, and to stimulate archaeological research into this era.

After centuries of Christian exclusivism, the Moorish presence has also re-established itself on the Peninsula. Over the past decades, Spain has developed from an emigration to an immigration country. A vast proportion of the migrant population consists of North Africans ('Moors'). Relations between these immigrants and the Spaniards continue to be dominated by ethno-religious images which have developed through the ages. Only a few years ago, North African agricultural workers in Catalonia who were threatened with expulsion protested against this decision by occupying a church for several days. The Aliens Act of 1 July 1985 (Ley Orgánica 7/1985), which dealt with the problem of illegal immigration, contains elements that are reminiscent of *casticismo*. While this law provides for facilities or preferential treatment for a whole range of categories of foreigners, it is also noticeable that it implicitly recognizes the incompatibility of the Muslim with a Spanish identity. The criterion on which the right to preferential treatment is founded, is the supposed greater adaptability of certain categories of foreigners to Spanish society and culture because of their identity or cultural affinity. The foreigners in question are predominantly from former Spanish colonies[28]. It is striking that, despite the long historical contacts with Islam and the many years that Morocco was a Spanish protectorate, the text of the law does not recognize a cultural affinity with either Muslims or Moroccans. Nor does it expect from them a smooth assimilation to the Spanish way of life.

It is evident from the commentaries on this law in the press - especially with regard to its implications for the Muslim populations of Ceuta and Melilla - that *casticismo* has remained important to the Spaniard for the interpretation of his relation to other ethnic communities. Here are some examples:

> 'In stead of applying an Afro-Spanish nationality law on everyone, we have invented a new 'limpieza de sangre': The Aliens Act' (Juan Pando Despierto, 'La política española en Africa. ¿Perpetuidad, residuo o exilio?' in El País, 29 Dec. 1995).
>
> 'And looking back even further in time, in search of historical nightmares, the expulsion of the Spanish Jews during the reign of the Catholic Kings and the expulsion of the Moriscos under Hapsburg rule are but modest points of comparison for the policy of *'limpieza de sangre'* and *'cristianismo viejo'* which the Government appears to want to introduce in Melilla' (El País, 17 Dec. 1985).
>
> 'Here is a discriminatory policy with racist traits, which is, moreover, rooted in a policy of *'limpieza de sangre'* whereby religion is associated with race' (Teresa Losada, 'La ley de extranjería y la situación de los marroquíes en España' in *Encuentro islamo-cristiano*, Madrid, no.167, March 1986).

Despite the protest from progressive quarters, there is no doubt that the idea expressed in this text of law concurs with the conviction of the average Spaniard, for whom being a Christian is still the essence of his ethno-national identity and who continues to assign a biological meaning to this religious identity. A reader's letter to El País (20 April 1990) contained the following definition: 'To be a Catholic means to be baptized and, even though one might not be practising, to be able to demonstrate that one's parents believed in the sacrament'. The fact that this 'biological Catholicism'[29] is still so strong perhaps explains why sociological surveys indicate such a high percentage of Roman Catholics, which is in contrast to the relatively low degree of religious praxis and belief in the foundations of the Roman Catholic doctrine. F. Lannon (1987: 34) mentions that, in the 1970s, 84% of Spaniards defined themselves as believers, and the author adds: 'For many Spaniards, however, belief in God and self-definition as Catholics coexisted peacefully with total neglect of the basic Catholic obligations of attending Sunday Mass and receiving sacraments once a year'[30].

In an extensive sociological survey of Spanish schoolchildren, 76% of the youngsters defined themselves as Catholics, of which more than half said they were not practising (Calvo Buezas 1995: 895-896).

*Casticismo* continues to be central to Spanish ethnic thinking. Conversations amongst Spaniards about the ethnic make-up of the Spaniard usually revolve around the different interpretations of the Islamic occupation (invasion by North Africans or Islamic revolution by autochthons), the process of repopulation after the Reconquista (by pure Spanish Northerners and Europeans or, by contrast, with a preservation of the Jewish-Moorish population) and the policy of ethnic cleansing from the era of the Catholic Kings. The Spaniard's lasting concern about *limpieza* has, for that matter, stamped its mark on historical scholarship. Américo Castro quite correctly points out that, until very recently, Spanish historiography appeared to be subject to a purity statute. In *De la edad conflictiva* (1972), Castro tries to demonstrate to which great extent Spanish historiography has been affected by *casticismo* values, and he earnestly requests that 'we should not subject the history of Spain to a statute of purity' (Castro 1972: 106). According to Américo Castro, Spanish historians have fallen victim to an internal 'psychological repression', namely the fear of 'Islamizing' the history of the nation (Castro 1983: 71).

The fact that the 'Moorish' chapter of Spanish history in particular was, to the extent that it threatened the ethnic purity itself, affected by an extremely subjective Spanish historiography is demonstrated very clearly by James T. Monroe in *Islam and the Arabs in Spanish Scholarship (Sixteenth Century to the present)* (1970). The image of the 'Moor' in the Spanish ethnic consciousness is responsible for a great deal of bias in Spanish historiography[31].

The emancipation of Spanish thinkers and scholars from the mental framework of *casticismo* in their reflection upon the Spanish people is a slow and as yet uncompleted process. The first Spanish thinker to make a concession with regard to the influence of the Moor on the Spanish identity is Ramiro de Maeztu in his work *Defensa de la Hispanidad*, dating from 1934[32]. Up until then, the Moorish and Jewish contribution to the ethnogenesis of the Spaniard had been systematically denied or obscured. As recently as 1921, Ortega y Gasset wrote that the 'Arabs' had not been an essential element in the genesis of the Spanish nationality[33]. Oddly enough it was Claudio Sánchez Albornoz, of all people, who reacted against this contention in 1929 by arguing that 'the Castilian psychology had slowly taken shape in the course of the age-long struggle against the Moor' (quoted in Gómez-Martínez 1975: 45). Sánchez Albornoz would later renounce this position. In *España, un enigma histórico* he wrote that 'the Arabic and the Jewish element had no - or at most a very minimal - influence on the genesis of the Spaniard' (quoted in Araya 1983: 59). Américo Castro's opinion developed in the opposite direction. While this author ignored the Moorish influence on the Spanish ethnogenesis in his earliest works, he later adopted the view initially held by Sánchez Albornoz (Araya 1983: 61). It appears that Castro too had to free himself of the mental framework of *casticismo*[34].

Despite this positive development, Spanish historiography remains strongly ethnically oriented and it devotes a lot of energy to 'blood analyses'. The ideologists of ethnicist movements as well as professional historians are concerned with determining the proportion of pure Old Christian blood to *converso* blood, both at a regional level (Basque provinces, Andalusia, etc.) and nationally. Efforts are made to establish the most accurate picture of the numerical presence and the exact origin of the Islamic occupiers; the origin and distribution of those who repopulated Andalusia; the demographic proportions of Christians, Moors and Jews; the precise impact of the measure of 1609 etc. According to some Spanish historians, these questions are important, not only from a purely historical point of view, but also because of their relevance to anthropological research into the present-day population of Spain[35].

Concern about purity of blood was the driving force behind the rise of peripheral nationalisms, especially Basque nationalism. And *casticismo* also remains the basis of the ethnic doctrines in these regional nationalisms. Basque nationalism developed at the end of the 19th century. It sprang from Carlism, a reactionary movement which, at the beginning of the century, had fought against the abolition of the Inquisition, because it recognized in this institution the only guarantee for the preservation of Spain's Old Christian purity. In historical Basque nationalism, the Spaniard is conceived as the opposite of the Basque. While the Basque is purely Old Christian, the Spaniard is the product of interbreeding with Jews and Moors, and as such he poses a threat to the original religious purity of the Basque.

In other peripheral nationalisms too one encounters the contradistinction of Christians and Moors. The regional ethno-nationalisms have in common that they all lay claim on a pure, Old Christian origin. The regional myth of origin is either situated in the pre-Islamic era or it consists of a denial of an Islamic presence on the territory. On taking into account the ethnic consciousness of the different regions, one notices how Iberia is intersected by a number of imaginary borders, whereby each region sets its own purity against the tainted, more 'Moorish' nature of the rest of the Peninsula. From a regional point of view, these ethnic borders are represented by a concrete geographic boundary. In the eyes of the Asturian, the mountain pass of Pajares, which separates Asturia from Castile, is the dividing line between the 'pure Spaniards' and the 'Moors'. And according to the Castilians, the Spanish-Moorish border coincides with the Despeñaperros or 'la Mariánica' (the border region between Castile and Andalusia). The Catalans regard the Ebro as the dividing line between 'Europe' and 'Africa'[36]. In Galician nationalism, the geographic isolation of this region is regarded as a clear enough separation with the more 'Moorish' Spain[37].

Andalusia, on the other hand, is faced with a dilemma. If this region appointed itself as Old Christian, there would be insufficient elements to legitimize Andalusian nationalism. Andalusia would be no more than '*Castilla Novísima*', an addition to Castile. In order to be able to confirm the historical and biological continuity as well as the originality of the Andalusian people, this region cannot but recognize the 'Moorish' influence on the particular blood pattern of the community and defend it. To this end, one must prove that, despite the age-long policy of ethnic cleansing, Moorish blood has not disappeared entirely from the region. In its search for traces of *converso* blood, Andalusian nationalism will seize upon each indication of incomplete ethnic cleansing in the past and try to maximize it. In the national historiography of Spain, by contrast, such indications are minimized because they are a threat to the supposed ethnic purity of the nation[38].

It certainly appears that in Spain the peripheral nationalisms that lean towards the 'casticist' frame of reference have been most successful. Basque nationalism developed from an extreme *casticismo*, as a result of which it could count on a strong identification by the Basque people. Consequently, the political breakthrough of Basque nationalism was not a long time coming. Andalusian nationalism, on the other hand, presents itself as anti-*casticismo* and clashes with established ethnic values. This makes the political and social breakthrough of Andalusian ethno-nationalism extremely difficult to realize, to the extent that one can still speak of a 'nationalism without nationalists'[39].

*Casticismo* has also continued to be important as an identification framework in the relationship between Spain and Europe. The extreme concern for '*limpieza de sangre*' and the strict control by the Inquisition on the orthodoxy of ideas and actions has, from the 16th century onwards, created a cleavage between Spain and Europe. For fear of an erosion of Spanish Christian purity, 'casticist' Spain cut itself off entirely from the revolutionary tendencies that took shape in Europe during the Reformation and later during the Enlightenment.

This stagnation or introversion - labelled by Ortega as '*tibetanización*' - was responsible for the creation of a rather negative image of Spain in Europe. According to this image, the Spaniard is typically a religious fanatic and intolerant; traits which by European tradition are associated with Islamic civilization. In the 'Black Legend', Spain is characterized by Europe with 'Moorish' (African/Islamic) stereotypes. This view is expressed in the famous phrase of Alexandre Dumas, that Africa begins on the other side of the Pyrenees.

While 'Europe' has, in the meantime, perhaps formed a more favourable picture of Spain, the 'Black Legend' has continued to weigh heavily on the Spaniard's self-perception in his relation to Europe. Julián Marías (1987: 206) observes that only few Spaniards are indifferent to the 'Black Legend', and he emphasizes its negative effects on the Spaniard's self-esteem and on Spain's international relations. The strong sense of *casticismo* of the Spaniard keeps alive his awareness of the fact that the prolonged contact with Islam has raised doubts in Europe as to his Old Christian origin. The fear of being branded as a 'Moor' by Europe is still relevant today (see also Vilar 1982: 231). Here is an example:

At the conclusion of the Spanish chairmanship of the European Community towards the end of June 1989, a balance was drawn up on the French television channel TF-1. Criticism was directed at the Spaniard's conception of time, which was felt to be 'less European': The

Spaniards appeared to be less concerned about sticking to schedules for meetings, which had led to some irritation amongst the European partners. Barely three months later, at the end of September, the Moroccan King, Hassan II, paid a three-day official visit to Spain. A constant theme in the Spanish press was the 'different conception of time' of the sovereign. The irritation that delays had caused amongst Spaniards was, at the same time, regarded as evidence of Spain's European character as opposed to that of the 'African' guest. El País (28 Sep. 1989) wrote that "the importance that the Spanish attach to punctuality does not correspond to the image that the Moroccans have of Spain as a 'Mediterranean country that is more African than European'".

## 4. *Convivencia*: An open possibility

We have previously pointed out that Spanish historiography has been coloured by *casticismo*. For a long time, the inherent prejudice of *casticismo* hampered reflection upon the originating of the Spanish as an ethnic group. Castro (1987: iii) regards the lack of insight on the part of the Spaniard into the process of his own ethnogenesis as a 'peculiar and painful anomaly'. This point of view is incorrect. On the contrary, one could argue that the fact that the Spaniard is able to distance himself from the mental framework of *casticismo* in the analysis of his ethnogenesis is a sign that the ethnic identification of the Spaniard with *casticismo* values has entered a regressive phase.

Contemporary progressive Spain is undoubtedly making efforts to break with the 'casticist' identity. Partly as a reaction to the historical sense of guilt towards the Islamic world, Spain is trying to adopt a more positive view on this world. A number of institutions -including some within the Spanish Roman Catholic Church[40] - have devoted themselves to a dialogue between Christianity and Islam, and oppose the negative image of the Moor which has prevailed in Spain. At a political level, the will to a historical rectification is taking shape. A good example of this is the recognition of Islam as a '*religión de notorio arraigo en España*' (religion that has 'taken root' in Spain) on 14 July 1989[41]. At the official start of negotiations between the Spanish Islamic community and the Spanish State on 11 October of the same year, the Minister of Justice gave a remarkable speech which expressed the power of the historical consciousness and its decisive influence on present relations of Spain with the Islamic world[42]. Also at a political level, Spain announced in 1986 on its entry into the European Union that it would give attention to the rapprochement between Europe and the Arab world[43]. The historical era of *convivencia* is a point of reference for Spain's possible peace mission in the political relations between the Western (Christian), the Jewish and the Arab (Islamic) world. The Madrid Peace Conference of 1991 is a symbol of the new policy of *convivencia* that Spain is pursuing.

Ethnic questions are not subject to the laws of determinism. However unshakeable and essential an ethnic identity may appear to the members of the ethnic group, there is, in reality, more room for manoeuvre than often assumed. An ethnic identity is not innate, but is passed on from generation to generation through socialization. Therefore the possibility of embarking on a new course in inter-ethnic relations always remains open.

On studying Spanish history, it becomes apparent that Spanish ethnicism did not necessarily have to lead to the exclusion of the ethnically different. Though it is impossible to weigh up in an objective way all the factors that contributed to the historical purges (such as the edicts expelling Jews in 1492 and Moriscos in 1609), it has by now become clear that history could at any time have taken another course. This probably explains why the study of Spanish heterodoxy by Menéndez Pelayo - despite the conviction of this scholar that Spain could not possibly be the breeding ground for heterodox tendencies - turned out to be such a bulky work, consisting of no less than eight volumes.

The preservation of an ethnically pluralistic society implies that there continue to be common ethnic values and symbols that create a bond between the different communities. This, in turn, may imply a deliberate manipulation of the respective ethnic myth-symbol complexes (A.D. Smith) or the ethnic genealogy. There are ample examples in Spanish history of experiments that went against the current of Old Christian exclusivism and searched for forms of symbiosis and synthesis that would make a multi-ethnic society possible. The Spanish sixteenth century is not just the century of ethnic intransigence, but also saw the emergence of an interesting countercurrent, i.e. illuminism or *alumbradismo*.

The illuminati searched for a new Christian ethic, with a new system of moral values, based on a more interiorized spirituality and an ecumenical concept of God (God as saviour of all believers, irrespective of their ethno-religious origins)[44]. From the Morisco side too a rapprochement was sought between Islam and Christianity, as is evident from the falsification of the Plomos del Sacromonte. Nineteenth-century Spanish Krausism and the subsequent Institución Libre de Enseñanza[45] were a continuation of the above-mentioned sixteenth-century initiatives. So the policy of Old Christian exclusivism and fundamentalism that Spain pursued for centuries was certainly not the result of a social consensus. Unanimity with regard to Spain's ethno-religious policy may be generally accepted in conservative thought, but it is not based on fact according to modern historical research (See, among others, Kamen, 1986; Márquez Villanueva, 1984).

## 5. How does 'casticism' survive?

The preservation of an ethnic identity through the ages is, first and foremost, connected with the mythical and symbolic character of ethnicity. According to Anthony D. Smith (1992) an ethnic community can be expected to survive as long as the 'myth-symbol complex' is passed on by successive generations. This does not mean that the culture of the people in question remains unchanged. The retention of the 'myth-symbol complex' is linked with the retention of a feeling of uniqueness and originality, and the idea that the community has some mission to accomplish. Many ethnic communities have a myth of 'ethnic election'. As regards Spain, the conditions that A.D. Smith believes to contribute to ethnic survival are abundantly present. Ethnicist Spain has always been convinced that the Spanish are a people chosen by God with a Christian mission to fulfil on earth. In a more secularized version, the myth of ethnic election continues to make itself felt in the European 'mission' of Spain and in the belief that Spain is the repository of the spiritual values of European civilization.

A second factor that has definitely contributed to the persistence of the framework of *casticismo* is the entwining of ethnicity and religion. One notices all across the world that, when an ethnic identity is principally based on a religious criterion, ethnic consciousness is prevalent and ethnic contradictions are persistent. To interfere with the ethnic identity of such communities is to interfere with their world view. To this day, the Spaniard experiences ethnicity and religion as related concepts. The average Spaniard will try and understand ethnic conflicts anywhere in the world in terms of religious differences. Linguistic differences between two ethnic communities are regarded to be of subordinate importance. Quite a few of our Spanish informants find it difficult to recognize the Basques as a separate ethnic community; to them the Spanish-Basque conflict is essentially a linguistic issue. They interpret the Belgian divide between Flemings and Walloons in exactly the same terms.

Conflicts among Europeans (whereby 'Europeans' stands for 'Christians') are soluble and are not conceived as ethnic conflicts, in contrast to religious conflicts, which are referred to in popular speech as 'racial conflicts'.

Thirdly, the close identification of the Spaniard with the ideal of *casticismo* is, without any doubt, also a consequence of the ethnic organization of society during the era of *convivencia* and the institutionalization of ethnicity in Spain at the time of the *limpieza de sangre*. If ethnic belonging is the organizational principle of a society and determines the social position of the individual, all are compelled to define themselves ethnically. The repercussions of ethnic organization on the ethnic consciousness cannot be emphasized enough. Ethnicity is more than the fight for material interests. It is also concerned with the protection of one's personality; with an aspect of identity. If precisely that aspect of an identity has taken a central position as a result of the ethnic organization of a society, it is logical that, even after a reform of that society, the individual will continue to be sensitive to any threat to the ethnic identity.

The concept of 'ethnic socialization' appears to us to be important in this respect. The contradiction between Moors and Christians still abounds the world in which the Spaniard grows up, not only in art and architecture, but also in village life with its local folklore, legends and sayings that refer explicitly to these contradictions, and, more subtly, in the vernacular with its often metaphorical usage of the terms *cristiano* and *moro*. Education plays an important part in the ethnic socialization of the Spanish youth. History teaching cannot but take a position on Spanish ethnicity and *casticismo*. At home, on the streets, in bars, in the media, at conferences and workshops; the Spaniard is always occupied with the question of his ethnic roots, including the relationship between Christians and Moors. The contradiction between Christians and Moors is a central theme in Spanish rites of passage. Baptism is of great symbolic importance and signifies the attribution of a Christian identity and the acceptance of the child into the community by a denial of it being a 'Moor'. This correlation finds expression in the Spanish saying that 'he who has not been baptized is a Moor'. At the barracks of Ceuta, the customary way to rag novices, who usually come from the Peninsula and who, despite never having met a 'Moor', still carry with them the historic image of the ethnic adversary, is to send them to the city refuse dump at night. Much to the amusement of the seniors, the novices would panic and flee the 'Moors' who would be scavenging the dump for usable objects and food for their survival.

Finally, we should like to point out that the ethnic attitude of the Spanish in terms of a Christian-Moorish boundary is perpetuated by the geographical location of Spain. From a geopolitical point of view, Spain still finds itself on the boundary between Christians and Moors. In a Europe without internal borders, Spain has the difficult task of guarding the Christian-Moorish border crossing, while the current socioeconomic situation in Spain holds a great attraction for people in Morocco.

There is now a trend amongst left-wing, progressive Spaniards and within the peripheral nationalist movements to reject the existence of the Spaniards as an ethnic community. They refuse to speak of 'Spain' as an ethnic reality and prefer to use the term '*Estado español*' (Spanish State), a political entity without an ethnic foundation[46]. This substitute term has been so widely accepted that even 'national' politicians increasingly refer to the '*Estado español*' in stead of '*Spain*', a word which has almost reactionary connotations. Contemporary

Spanish thinkers too have expressed doubts about the possibility of ethnically defining the word '*español*' and it is generally accepted that the Spanish people are, in essence, characterized by a diversity which cannot be understood in one word[47].

Despite this scepticism and the justifiably critical self-analysis to which the Spanish intelligentsia subjects itself, the 'biological' antagonism between Islam and Christianity, which we have in this chapter analyzed thoroughly through the ages, has undeniably led to the persistence of an ethnic matrix and a symbolic frame of reference by means of which the division between 'us' and 'the others' is constructed and perpetuated; plasmic, not deterministic, but difficult to either dismantle or remodel in course of just one generation, because unconsciously this matrix remains at work in small details that continue to surface unexpectedly during socialization. And this cannot be altered merely by an intellectual discourse.

*Notes*

1. Or possibly three categories: Christians, Jews, and Moors; see Caro Baroja (1978 b, III: 174).

2. 'To be a good Christian' means to comply with the sociocultural code (see also Freeman 1968: 42).

3. See Caro Baroja 1985: 108, 143; Ladero Quesada 1979: 35; Domínguez Ortiz 1983: 53. In the Islamic era some of these very elements were, in fact, attributed to the Christians. (see Caro Baroja 1990: 89).

4. In her book entitled '*Santa María del Monte*' (1986: 268-271), Ruth Behar demonstrates how the two mythic eras are intertwined in the collective memory.

5. The historical confusion of the different moments of contact between Spaniards and Moors is also evident in the explanatory models of the vaqueiros de Alzada, a small minority in northern Spain, with regard to their supposed Moorish origin (see Cátedra Tomás 1989).

6. For a description of this term, see Stallaert 1996 and 1998.

7. See, among others, Castro 1987: 193; Payne 1984: 11.

8. See García Morente 1943: 70-71; Araya 1983: 219. Cf. Julián Marías (1987: 417): "*los demás países europeos eran cristianos, pero no consistían en ello*".

9. See, among others, Suárez Fernández 1981: 557; Lea 1983, II: 160-162.

10. See Kamen 1986.

11. See Boxer 1974.

12. See Márquez Villanueva 1984.

13. See Castro 1974: 252-253.

14. See Castro 1987: 81; 1987: i-ii, 23, 89, 197; 1972, b: 15, 239, 240; etc.

15. Le Flem et al. 1984: 157; Monsalvo Antón 1985: 213; Menéndez Pidal, *Historia de España*, part XIII, volume I; Cardaillac 1991: 50-51; Arié 1987: 178-181; Suárez Fernández, in Moxó y Ortiz de Villajos 1984: XLI.

16. The structure of the caste system is, after all, incompatible with a policy of conversion. Outspoken proselytism would have undermined the pillars of society, as would later become apparent in the *converso*-issue. The two essential features on which the entire system was founded were respect for other religions and faithfulness to one's own religion. Apostasy and proselytism are forms of social behaviour that clash with the principles of a caste system, because they conflict with the birth-ascribed status of the individual. Such transgressions were therefore regarded as a source of social conflict and were punishable by law. Officially, conversion to Christianity was accepted but, in reality, the convert would have to contend with social condemnation of his behaviour.

17. Sicroff 1960: 140; see also Domínguez Ortiz 1985: 25; Lea 1983, II: 158, Menéndez Pidal 1989, XIX: 416.

18. The fact that according to the absolute *limpieza*-criterion there were hardly any Spaniards with pure blood left, was used as an argument by those who were in favour of reforming the *limpieza*-statutes (Caro Baroja 1978 b, II: 331; Asensio 1976: 158).

19. Sicroff 1960: 191; Caro Baroja 1978 b, II: 332; Revah 1971: 291-292; Chauchadis 1984: 127-128; Castro 1974: 251; Bataillon 1966: 60.

20. Revah (1971: 295-296) refers to the striking example of don Luis de Mercado, a member of the Council of the King, who, after two enquiries with a favourable outcome, was refused *limpieza* following a third enquiry prompted by a new appointment. The refusal was based on 'rumours' about the Jewish descent of a grandfather.

21. See Sicroff 1960: 215.

22. See Cardaillac 1977: 96.

23. See Juan de Pineda, *Diálogos familiares de la agricultura cristiana*, quoted in Chauchadis 1984: 172; see also Caro Baroja 1978 a: 490.

24. This according to a book dating from 1726 containing instructions on how to initiate children into the secret of their ancestry (see Domínguez Ortiz 1988: 152).

25. See Caro Baroja 1978 b, II: 286; Domínguez Ortiz 1985: 16-17.

26. As regards the role of *casticismo* in the development of the peripheral nationalisms in Spain, see Stallaert 1996 and 1998.

27. For a more detailed discussion, see Stallaert 1996.

28. The Law states the following: 'Although the Law governing the Rights and Liberties of foreigners is not the appropriate place to enter upon the issue of acquisition of nationality, it is on the other hand the appropriate place *to advance the possible circumstances of which one may assume that they will lead to a higher degree of assimilation to the Spanish way of life*'; 'From this line of argument follows a concern of the Law with the preferential treatment of Iberian Americans, Portuguese, Filipinos, inhabitants of Andorra and Equatorial Guinea, Sephardic Jews and migrants from the town of Gibraltar, *as these people meet the requirement of presumed cultural affinity and identity that entitles them to this consideration*' (italics supplied).

29. This term is taken from J. Jiménez Lozano 1966: 59.

30. Cf. López-Pintor and Wert Ortega 1982: 11.

31. See also Glick 1991: 12; Caro Baroja 1986: 165.

32. See Gómez-Martínez 1975: 26-27.

33. Ortega 1984: 129.

34. In *La realidad histórica de España* (1987: iv) Castro concedes that, for a long time, he was guilty of '*europeización retrospectiva*', viz. not recognizing the specificity of Spain within the Christian world as a result of its Moorish/Jewish legacy.

35. See Domínguez Ortiz and Vincent 1978: 247.

36. See, among others, Horst 1985; Trías Vejarano 1975. Colomer 1986; Solé 1980 and 1981.

37. See, among others, Máiz 1984, a and b; Bobillo 1981.

38. For a more comprehensive discussion of Andalusian ethno-nationalism, see Stallaert, 1996.

39. J.M. Cuenca Toribio (1991: 30) uses this expression in a discussion of historical Andalusian nationalism.

40. The efforts made by Emilio Galindo Aguilar, director of the Centro Darek-Nyumba (Madrid), first spring to mind in this respect.

41. The Jewish religion was recognized as '*religión de notorio arraigo*' in December 1984. During negotiations on the acquisition of this status, the Islamic community of Spain put particular emphasis on the historical role of Islam in the Spanish ethnicity process ('Islam is one of the religions at the basis of the historical personality of Spain'; 'our tradition and culture are inseparably linked to the religious foundations that have given shape to the deepest essence of the Spanish people', in: *Encuentro islamo-cristiano*, no. 222, Oct. 1990, p.17).

42. See *Encuentro islamo-cristiano*, no. 213-214, Jan.-Feb. 1990, p.23.

43. See *Historia 16*, no. 133, volume XIII, May 1987.

44. See, among others, Selke 1980.

45. See, among others, Lannon 1987: 39-40.

46. In a recent book on anthropology (Frigolé, et al. 1983), the authors systematically refer to their Spanish readers as 'readers of the Spanish State', carefully avoiding the terms 'españoles' (Spaniards) and 'España' (Spain).

47. See, among others, Racionero (1987: 60): "We are in essence diversity and that is precisely why we create a problem when we try and grasp this essence in one single notion, that of the 'Spaniard'. He who wishes to define this state of 'being a Spaniard' creates an insoluble problem, the quadrature of the circle, a problem that one will not be able to solve by any means. For how can one define in a single word what is by definition diverse, changeable and transforms before our very eyes like a chameleon? This is impossible".

# Chapter VII:

# Indigenous and Immigrant Ethnicities: Differences and Similarities

### Johan Leman

## 1. What do we understand by ethnicity?

Some authors (Bell 1975: 156-157; Patterson 1975: 305) have pointed out that the use of the terminology about ethnicity is not always equally clear. Authoritative anthropologists, sociologists, and psychologists, drawing on a wide-ranging knowledge of the field, have repeatedly tried to grasp the core of ethnicity so that the first priority for some time to come will not be to redo this work. Nevertheless, it is important that we, at least for our own use, clearly state what we mean by ethnicity in our research, without, however, wanting to generate the illusion that we envision the only "right definition" (cf. Chapman, McDonald, and Tonkin 1989: 11).

With ethnicity, we mean, (1), a "subjective, symbolic or emblematic use ... of any aspect of culture, in order to differentiate ... from other groups" (Brass 1991: 19), (2), on the basis of "a feeling of continuity with the past, a feeling that is maintained as an essential part of one's self-definition" (De Vos 1975: 17), (3) providing "reservoirs for renewing humane values. Ethnic memory is thus future, not past, oriented" (Fischer 1986: 176), and (4) whereby it is not "the cultural stuff that it encloses" that fundamentally decides what is involved in the we-consciousness but "the ethnic boundary that defines the group" (Barth 1969: 15).

Ethnic frontiers are social frontiers. However, this need not yet mean that the existence of social frontiers is sufficient to explain the generation itself of ethnic frontiers nor that this offers a sufficient explanation for the concrete filling in (for example, the degree and content of possible antagonism) of the ethnic tradition in a particular group

Edmund Leach (1954) and Fredrik Barth (1969) were the first to stress the dynamic approach to the ethnic consciousness. A group of people with the same ethnicity consciousness defines itself only indirectly in terms of its own characteristics. It is done in the first place in comparison with those that are ethnically different. At the same time, this implies processes of boundary maintenance and boundary manipulation. Differences of opinion about the common boundaries and about the markers between neighbors of different ethnicity, the existence of border guards, and a frequent variation of cultural and possibly linguistic elements within the ethnic group are thus legion (LeVine and Campbell 1972: 85-99).

All the previous chapters, about "immigrant ethnicities" as well as "indigenous ethnicities" have shown that, in practice, it is fully sterile to opt either for a primordialistic or a circumstantialistic starting point in the explanation of ethnicity. The two approaches complement each other (Spicer 1971; Drummond 1980; Smith 1981; McKay 1982; Scott 1990; Wilson 1993). In the present debate (Poutignat and Streiff-Fenart 1995: 143), it is a matter of again introducing content into the ethnicity theories without relapsing into the substantialism of previously. Therefore, this is what we have tried to do.

We think that the content fillings are category-bonded and also involve "matrices", which, however, leave open a large margin for an arbitrariness of real content fillings.

## 2. Two major categories of ethnicity

There is no such thing as one kind of ethnicity. What Fischer has ascertained for American ethnic identities is also true for our research, namely "that these ethnicities constitute only a family of resemblances, that ethnicity cannot be reduced to identical sociological functions, that it is a process of interreference between two or more cultural traditions, and that these dynamic mechanisms of intercultural knowledge provide reservoirs for renewing humane values" (Fischer 1986: 176). Even though the search for something like ethnic matrices that have germinated in the past always occupies an important place in our research, a clear distinction must be made between at least two categories of ethnicity, a category of immigrant ethnicities and a category of indigenous ethnicities. Moreover, both categories are characterized by a diversity in creation modalities.

For the immigrant ethnicities, a number of creation modalities among West European Mediterranean allochthons are assembled in chapter 2. It is the dynamics over three generations that lead here to specific forms of ethnicity per generation − actually often more forms of sub-ethnicity − that can be understood in terms of one single logic. At the same time, however, this is crossed by processes of hybridization and of supra-ethnicity.

> This trend towards "pure homogenicity", however, is nowhere realized, for it is simultaneously traversed by three opposing dynamics of a hybridizing nature. They are: (1) the so-called homogeneous cultures already in fact containing themselves elements of hybridism; (2) the hyphenization among the allochthons; and (3) a creolizing cultural continuum. (Leman 1999b: 351)

> In these specific processes of transformation, we refer to the religions as 'modulators', that is, they shape and alter the socio-ethnic processes at play in pluri-ethnic cities; these operate by responding to supply and demand among people located in a specific socio-ethnic and generational position and come into contact with religions on the ground. (Leman 1999a: 218-219)

For the indigenous ethnicities, one notes that the matrices can either be clearly traced back to one particular period in the distant past (see the chapter by Stallaert) or gradually take form during a limited number of long-lasting and strongly interacting periods (see the chapter by Van de Vijver). The historical modeling of such a matrix is never definitive but is always subject to revision. The filling in can take place throughout the entire history with some arbitrariness (Roosens 1989: 160-161).

A situation has also been described in which the two major categories of ethnicity merge, namely in the chapter by Ghequière.

Finally, there is a chapter by Chang, which is interesting from our point of view for two reasons, firstly because it describes a precursor of forms of involuntary immigration that will occur in a multitude of situations outside the Western context in the next ten years and, secondly, because at the same time it implicitly raises the question as to whether the rationality of a Western ethnic construct is in fact the right way of explaining the "process of interference between two or more cultural traditions" that ensue.

It should be possible to distinguish the circumstances in which the categories and forms of ethnicity are awakening, leaving aside whether each manifestation must be called ethnic to the same degree (Moerman 1994: 130-133). It may be stimulating for future anthropological research to integrate more and more non-Western categories in the study of non-Western ethnicity.

Our search, consequently, consists of determining which are the specific creation modalities and forms that occur strictly within each of both categories.

## 3. History and "matrices"

Many anthropologists agree that an involvement of not only political and economic but also cultural history can be very illuminating in the analysis of the anthropological "present" (Eriksen 1993: 96). But the question also arises, of course, of the epistemological status of the anthropological knowledge of the past.

No anthropologist disputes that the subjective and time-bonded contribution of the historiographer-anthropologist is part of the interpretation of the past that is studied. That there is at least a mutual implication of past and present is not doubted: "Symbolic action is a duplex compound made up of an inescapable past and an irreducible present" (Sahlins 1985: 152); "every fact that has been recorded and is today assumed to be historically valid is shaped from conflicting imaginations, at once past and present" (De Certeau 1988: 11). It is a question of constantly new interpretation and re-interpretation: "history is an imprinting of the present onto the past" (Friedman 1994: 837). According to some, it is even a matter of continuous manipulation: "almost anything and everything are possible" (Roosens 1989: 161).

Where the opinions or accents diverge, what is involved is the vision of the possibility of transcending the present-bonded character of the historiographer and of the insight into history and implicitly the question whether, alongside the knowledge of "how does the present create the past?", one can also find an answer to "how did the past lead to the present?" (Chapman, McDonald and Tonkin 1989: 1)? History continues to work through in the present (Silverman 1979: 432). Is it possible to so study history that it does not appear as a pure succession of independent facts and interpretations that are only to be understood from an ever new present? "In many cases it is clear that group history has been fashioned so as to serve present needs, but this does not imply that anything goes" (Eriksen 1993: 93). A number of authors have made anthropological use of the "objective" in the past in function of an analysis of the present. "It is a hypothesis that existing structural relationships of a strong kind are not lightly abandoned," even Ardener writes (1989: 29). Grosby speaks about "historically evolving patterns of belief and action.

The individual participates in these given, a priori bounded patterns. The patterns are the legacy of history; they are tradition" (Grosby 1994: 164).

Le Goff specifies this by asking that special attention be given to these periods in the past in which communities have come in contact with each other (Le Goff 1977: 346). The great problem, of course, remains how one can compare situations from different times and places with each other (Armstrong 1982: 10).

In his study about the Maya-Q'eqchi' of Guatemala, with whom the monumental icon decor has been a matrix over time from which the various cultural and ethnic responses have arisen, Wilson speaks of "a monumental matrix carried forward from the past" (Wilson 1993: 135). Other authors find in a distant past a long-lasting matrix of ethnic-social interchanges that has led groups of people to position themselves with respect to each other in such a manner that it continued to make itself felt afterwards.

Thus, Armstrong sees "the frontier" between Islam and Christianity and the period of the *Reconquista* as the "mythomotor" of Spanish ethnogenesis (Armstrong 1982: 65-75), while Friedman, in his discussion of the origin of the modern nationalistic Greek identity points to the importance of the institutionalized interrelations between Christians and Muslims during the time of the Ottoman Empire and to the simultaneous antagonism between the Eastern and the Western churches, whereby Orthodoxy thereafter represented the "true" Christianity (Friedman 1992: 838).

These initial institutionalized matrices, which of themselves had nothing to do with ethnicity but rather with another kind of organizational principle (particularly of an "ascriptive affiliational religious" nature), are situated, in the case of historical ethnicity in periods before the Modern Period. From the outset, they were organizational principles in which, in later times, all kinds of memories, values, myths, and symbols came to settle, so that certain authors correctly began to speak of a "myth-symbol complex" as the core of this category of ethnic identity (Smith 1986: 15), others of "a mythomotor" (Armstrong 1982: 8-9). The "historical memories", in their turn, occur simultaneously with "specific historical forces". It makes the collectivities "subject to historical change and dissolution" (Smith 1991: 20).

"Ethnic communities can reasonably be said to have survived in something like their earlier forms, if successive generations continue to identify with some persisting memories, symbols, myths and traditions" (Smith 1992: 445). The great state nationalisms of the 19th and 20th centuries were an attempt to combine these mythical and emotional traditional forces that have developed fully, borne by a matrix from a far past, into a modern, cerebral concept of the state. With the post-modern ethnic nationalisms of the end of the 20th century, the movement is in the reverse direction, and state ideologies are projected on pre-modern matrices framed by reduced, elementary myths and symbols.

In the case of both the Spanish - North-African social and cultural mutual relationships, as seen from the Spanish viewpoint, and internal Spanish regionalism, and also in the case of the intercultural and social relationships between the Hungarians and Romanians in Transylvania, there is a clear application of the existence of "historical matrices", which have developed from centuries of mutual perceptions and confrontations dating back to pre-modern times. This kind of matrix underlies both autochthonous ethnicity and the nationalist movements that are characteristic of the modern and post-modern era in these countries.

## 4. The basically future oriented life of immigrants

It is clear that a long-lasting historical dimension is lacking in the case of a movement of integration among immigrants who mobilized themselves in a host country gradually, generally over three generations. Here, too, as regards ethnicity, it is always a matter of an interpreted (and possibly manipulated) affecting of a past back to a minimum of three generations in the case of a third or fourth generation. But, normally, in function of the nature of the integration, this cannot lead to one single, specific, enduring matrix that would permanently profile the relationship between autochthons and the allochthons toward each other.

Sometimes, what is involved here is a fragmentary low degree of ethnicity deriving from a piece of past history, that arrives at some symbolic expressivity (Gans 1979, 1994). In other cases, it is better structured and supported by a limited number of social institutions (places of worship, shops, schools) and some local leadership.

To the degree that, in the immigration situation, after generations, any enduring mutual positioning of the ethnic group type remains active, it goes back to matrices that belong in originally indigenous ethnicity, such as the relationship between Christianity and Islam or relationships of long-lasting colonial times (such as some relationships between "blacks" and "whites"). The sedimentation of institutional-religious diversity (such as that between Eastern Christian-Orthodox believers and Western Catholics) can to some extent continue to play a part in an urban immigration context, after several generations, in terms of the organisation of some aspects of social and family life.

This does not prevent one from speaking of various forms of immigrant ethnicity that correspond to specific models, depending on whether a first, second, third, or later generation is involved. Nor does it prevent this phenomenon, in view of the frequency with which immigrations will still continue to occur for decades, from continuing to contribute to the determination of the social agenda.

One striking aspect of these immigration patterns is that the communities involved actually act and think in an integration-oriented, which is to say a future-oriented way, so that long-lasting historical matrices are not developed (unless perhaps of the strictly religious kind in the case of some of these people), let alone a concern to preserve matrices dating from pre-modern times at all costs. Even among the Suryoye from South-East Turkey it is noticeable how certain distinctions from pre-modern times (in this case internal Christian schisms) are quite quickly suppressed to enable them to function more effectively in West-European society.

In the case of the Suryoye, one sees clearly how the matrix that determines their positioning with respect to themselves and "the other" (the other being the non-Christian, the Muslim, or the Christian who does not belong to their church) arose via a long-term process that goes back to the dividing line between Muslims and Christians at the time of the Ottoman Empire (with a complication due to the absorption of Kurdish social structures) and also between Eastern and Western Christians (with a new complication resulting from the intra-church divisions that are peculiar to the Christianity of this region in modern Southeast Turkey).

Because of the continuous pressure for Turkification, Kemalism of Ataturk, which no longer left a place for ethnic minorities, in spite of its secular character, pushed them ever further into a corner as a minority group, a product of the earlier Islamic millet system. This ultimately led them to emigrate and completely disappear from Southeast Turkey.

It shows us a group composed of clusters, in which a fragmented religion and a fragmenting social organization based on related foundations are strongly interwoven and reinforce each other. Their "indigenous ethnicity" is confronted with new challenges in the immigration situation, and one notes the first attempts at remodeling in the effort to transcend the mutual differences either by positioning themselves as a whole as "original" Christians with respect to the new "others" (i.e., the secularized Christian majority group) or by situating the mutual bond outside of the religious realm.

## 5. The central place of religion (and language) in the debate on both immigrant and indigenous ethnicities

The differing components from the definition of ethnicity (cf. Brass, De Vos, Fischer and Barth) used by us on the different fields in this study and the recurrent findings on the place of religion and language, are clearly applicable to most of the situations in this publication. In actual fact this does not matter so much for the situation of the KMT Yunnanese Chinese in Northern Thailand, and that should give us food for thought.

In the situation of the Magyars and ethnic Romanians in Transylvania e.g., one notes that the positioning of Christianity with respect to Islam from the time of the Ottoman Empire also has had a profound effect on the perception of both the Romanians and the Magyars. The collective memory of both population groups has it that they stopped the march of Islam and have played an important role for Christianity and for Western Europe.

But here, too, are also some intra-Christian divisions that have reinforced the mutual ethnic profiling. At the end of the 17th century, Eastern Orthodoxy was there a tolerated but discriminated-against religion with respect to the Catholicism, Calvinism, and Lutheranism supported by the Hungarian hegemony. A process was set in motion to Westernize Eastern Orthodoxy by means of transition to the Uniate Church with the same high status as the other three religions. But contrary to the intentions, a dynamic emerged that contributed to the rise of ethnic-Romanian nationalism in the 18th century.

As among the Suryoye, we observe that matrices were generated whereby ascriptive affiliational religion and pre-industrial rural organizational principles, albeit less compelling than the related type, determined the social structure for centuries. However, quite quickly state structures were mixed with them that have colored the interior frontiers between the residents of Transylvania with myths and symbols that came to live their own lives both toward the past (cf. the discussion of the right of primogeniture in Transylvania) and toward the future (cf. the discussion about who truly belongs to Europe).

What is striking among the Suryoye, the Magyars, and the ethnic Romanians is the reflection of their religious and mythical discussions on the status and the uniqueness of the language they use.

Deserving separate mention are the Transylvanian gypsies, who as yet seem to be weighed down under a negative identity, "the internalized evaluations of others" (Epstein 1978: 102). Groups in a special marginal position have difficulty in creating their own history so that it is also difficult for traces of "indigenous ethnicity" to develop.

In Spain and with the Spanish regionalisms, our last case of "indigenous ethnicity", it is amply demonstrated that, in a distant past, a socio-cultural matrix (casticism, cultural "purity of blood") can be found that up to the present is still giving form to the ethnic positioning of Spaniards both internally among themselves and exteriorly to non-Spaniards. The historicity of a number of Spanish institutions makes the matrix permanent, which, in its turn, has lead to a habitus and socialization praxis.

Noteworthy in indigenous ethnicity for the initial impetus, we are invariably compelled to look to periods before the Modern Period (thus before the rise of the modern nationalisms).

What are involved are matrices that arise in a social environment where people are born with a religious world view that is inherent to their family origins and environment at a time that such a unity, organized as a system, either is taken up by a whole that is also organized as a system that corresponds to the same seclusion or takes up into itself such an alien coherent system. In both cases, it is also necessary for the two systems to let each other exist in their autonomy but that rules are, nevertheless, worked out, generally by the stronger party, to regulate intercourse between them (marriage, commerce, political participation, change of religion).

The matrix, in fact, allows the minority group to continue itself on an historic-regressive level (in comparison with the new political situation) even though the times change and even though the broader social context is thoroughly shaken up. The minority group can reorganize its security on the regressive level in view of a cohesive approach of the future.

When such a matrix endures for centuries, whereby both the majority group and the minority group or groups can keep up their internal social relations without performing the adjustments required for a common management based on equal principles, then, for each of them, a projection space is created of myths, symbols, and emblems. These elements will traditionally support their own position both to justify their own greatness (in the case of a majority group) and to invoke a lost and in-the-future-to-be-recovered greatness (in the case of minority groups).

This leads to a complex in which religious commitment (the stories proper to a founding religion), its reflection on a specific language, and an image of society of the more broadly related type (Horowitz 1985: 57) from the time from before the rise of the great empires and state structures give content to a social positioning mechanism by which people define themselves as a group separate from "the others".

This is unconsciously passed on over the generations via the historicity of the institutions, the stories, the socialization, and the habitus of the group members.

Normally, this set of attitudes is not at the forefront in everyday life, in the work or family life that completely absorbs someone. It also is not expressed when someone is confronted with personal problems or encounters dysfunctions in his own personal environment. It is activated, however, when the group as a whole is confronted with a new social development involving social events that transcend it. This can be a social, political, or military conflict from the outside that is experienced as threatening or a social, cultural, institutional, or political increase of scale that is also seen as endangering the existing balance. This then leads to an activation of the matrix and to an actualizing reinterpretation of the complex of myths, symbols, and emblems.

Nothing pejorative is meant by the use of the term "regression", but rather something illusory. It is a regression to a previous stage because there the positive elements dominate or better because no negative elements, nothing alien, nothing evil can be found in it. Idealization of the past makes this possible. It may help restore or strengthen group cohesion in the present-day by getting people to face the future in this way from the viewpoint of a broadly-based dynamism.

With immigrant ethnicities, what is involved are also limited forms of valorization of elements from the past that, for the people involved, are experienced or "confessed" as not-alien, and this with a dynamic that reaches over three generations and transcends the groups of people taken up in it.

However, there is no space for the germination of an enduring matrix or for the rise of enduring myths, symbols, and emblems, except to the degree in which they, too, emigrated as indigenous ethnicity to the new situation, where they then, however, are taken up, in principle in a process of crumbling remodeling. As in the case of the indigenous ethnicities, religions also play a key regulatory part in the case of the immigrant ethnicities, certainly over three generations, where public interest in the language of origin, as the second important diacritic, usually declines after two generations - with a few notable exceptions that can be attributed to an organic multilingual social context (Paulston 1987; Leman 1990; Leman 1991). We have already pointed out that, primarily in metropolitan multiethnic settings, pluri-religiosity can intersect and partially coordinate the processes of ethnic homogenisation and cultural hybridisation from the second and third generation on.

On this point we can ask ourselves whether there are not two very obvious reasons why the ethnicity genesis among the KMT Yunnanese Chinese develops according to a somewhat different categorisation than is the case among the communities based on Western (Christian) and Islamic principles, namely the very different social and cultural role and interpretation of Chinese religiosity (Yang 1991) and the part played e.g. by Yin and Yang as structuring principles of Chinese thinking and social behaviour. This may be a warning for anthropologists that a different social interpretation of religiosity should perhaps also lead to a change in the way in which the ethnicity issue is approached within a particular community.

All this makes it clear that the development of the multi-ethnic (or multicultural) societies that arise from all kinds of immigration movements will, in the long run, be chiefly determined by the way in which structures and sedimentations of different religious institutions, which are imported with these movements, can continue to be used as a mobilisation factor.

The multicultural society that ensues from immigrations will essentially be a multi-ethnic society in which elements of multireligiosity interfere to a limited extent in the areas where this is allowed by social consensus.

## 6. 'Content' in ethnicity theories

> Poutignat and Streiff-Fenart (1995: 143) rightly point out that the task now facing us is to bring 'content' back into ethnicity theories, without lapsing into substantialism and without jeopardising the achievements of research according to the principals of Barth. (Bafekr & Leman 1999: 97)

We have already talked about an historical matrix in the case of indigenous ethnicity. We have just pointed out the place of religion and, secondarily, language where it concerns the articulation of ethnicity across a first, second, and third generation in immigrant ethnicity or in the structuring of metropolitan interethnicity, or even as prominent criteria for the expression of indigenous ethnicity.

There is clearly still more 'content' operative that pushes itself more strongly to the fore (alongside religion and language) than other potential cultural contents, namely family and kinship as symbolic structures. In a discussion of the community of Italo-Brussels Jehovah's Witnesses in the multiethnic metropolitan setting of Brussels, I noted:

> It is noticeable, more so than among the autochtonous JW, how in this community kinship is very much in evidence as a source of support and as a symbolic frame of reference. (Leman 1998: 225-226)

With the kinship symbolic, just as with the religious symbolic, we are close to the question of the origin of individuality and whoever pauses at this question is also directly confronted with the question about 'self' and 'otherness'. At the origin of the content and emotional orientations, of the import and the antagonistic character or not of the ethnicity, stands the pre-reflexive perception of the self and of the other that lies sedimented in a community in its socialisation processes and institutions.

Religion builds further on it. The languages are also instrumentalised from such a perspective. The kinship symbolic in its turn lends itself to concrete metaphorisation. Where necessary and possible, the historical matrices are activated by it.

All the parts of this publication show how complex the production schemas of the many forms of ethnogenesis are. Groups of people have many ways to express what they are and how they act, feel, and think. What anthropologists indicate by ethnicity interferes with this expression but in very divergent ways.

Its unraveling will still require a great deal of work. But, in the meantime, these articles confirm what has long been certain: as Horowitz has observed, we may never think in terms of a big-bang theory of ethnogenesis (Horowitz 1985: 70).

**REFERENCES**

**CHAPTER I**

Bafekr, S. & Leman, J. (1999) 'Highly-qualified Iranian immigrants in Germany: the role of ethnicity and culture', Journal of Ethnic and Migration Studies, 25(1), 95-112

Barth, F. (1969) Ethnic Groups and Boundaries: the Social Organisation of Culture Difference. Oslo, Bergen, Tromso: Universitetsforlaget

Guarnizo, L.E. (1994) 'Los Dominicanyorks: The Making of a Binational Society', The Annals of the American Academy, AAPSS, 533: 70-86

Hollinger, D. (1995) Postethnic America: Beyond Multiculturalism. New York: Basic Books

Leman, J. (1998) 'The Italo-Brussels Jehovah's Witnesses Revisited', Social Compass, 45(2): 219-226

Leman, J. (1999) 'Religions, Modulators in Pluri-Ethnic Cities: An Anthropological Analysis of the Relative Shift from Ethnic to Supra-Ethnic and Meta-Ethnic Faith Communities in Brussels', Journal of Contemporary Religion, 14(2): 217-231

Morin, E. (1987) Penser l'Europe. Paris: Gallimard

Nwolisa-Okanga, E.C. (1999) "Njepu Amaka" – It's good to migrate: white man's magic and ethnicity among the Igbo people of Eastern Nigeria. Leuven, Ph.D. thesis in the social and cultural anthropology

Roosens, E. (1994) 'The primordial nature of origins in migrant ethnicity', in Vermeulen, H. & Govers, C. (eds.) The Anthropology of Ethnicity: beyond 'Ethnic Groups and Boundaries'. Amsterdam: Het Spinhuis, 81-104

Scantlebury, E. (1995) 'Muslims in Manchester: The Depiction of a Religious Community', New Community, 21(3): 425-435

Van Broeck, A.-M. (1999) Transnationalisme bij Colombiaanse migranten: tussen Brussel en Medellin. Leuven, Ph. D. thesis in the social and cultural anthropology

**CHAPTER II**

Bafekr, S. & Leman, J. (1999) 'Highly-qualified Iranian immigrants in Germany: the role of ethnicity and culture', Journal of Ethnic and Migration Studies, 25(1): 95-112

Chang, Wen-Chin (1996) A preliminary study on the ethnic identification of the KMT Chinese in Northern Thailand, report in progress (typewritten)

162

Dwyer, C. and Meyer, A. (1996) 'The establishment of Islamic Schools', in Shadid, W.A.R. and van Koningsveld, P.S. (eds.) Muslims in the margin. Kampen, the Netherlands: Kok Pharos Publishing House, 218-242

Epstein, A.L. (1978) Ethos and identity. London: Tavistock Publications

Gitmez, A. and Wilpert, C. (1987) 'A micro-society or an ethnic community? Social organization and ethnicity amongst Turkish migrants in Berlin', in Rex, J. (ed.) Immigrant associations in Europe. Aldershot: Gower, 86-125

Handelman, D. (1977) 'The organization of ethnicity', Ethnic Groups, vol. 1, 187-200

Joly, D. (1987) 'Associations amongst the Pakistani population in Britain', in Rex, J. (ed.) Immigrant associations in Europe. Aldershot: Gower, 62-85

Kunz, E.F. (1973) 'The refugee in flight: Kinetic models and forms of displacement', International Migration Review, 7 (2): 125-164

Leman, J. (1979a) 'Jehovah's witnesses and immigration in Continental Western Europe', Social Compass XXVI(1), 41-72

Leman, J. (1979b) 'La deuxième génération des travailleurs migrants: fragmentés et non destructurés', Recherches Sociologiques X(2), 247-270

Leman, J. (1982) Van Caltanissetta naar Brussel en Genk. Leuven, Amersfoort: Acco

Leman, J. (1987) From challenging culture to challenged culture. Leuven: University Press

Leman, J. (1990) 'Bruselas y sus poblaciones mediterraneas: reflexiones etnograficas acerca de territorio e identidad', in Actas Simposio internacional de antropoloxia 'Identidade e Territorio', Consello da Cultura Galega, 47-60

Leman, J. and Gailly, A. (under the direction of) (1991) Thérapies interculturelles. Brussels: De Boeck Université

Leman, J. (1994) 'La etnicidad inducida, el racismo y la violencia de y hacia los inmigrantes en Europa Occidental', in Fernandez de Rota y Monter, Etnicidad y Violencia. La Coruña, 121-135

Leman, J., ed. (1995) Sans document: les immigrés de l'ombre. Brussels: De Boeck Université

Leman, J., ed. (1996) Allochtone godsdienstigheid in een grootstad. Brussels: Cultuur en Migratie, 1996-2

Leman, J. (1998) 'The Italo-Brussels Jehovah's Witnesses revisited: from first-generation religious fundamentalism to ethno-religious community formation', Social Compass, June (in press)

Leman, J. (1999a) 'Religions, Modulators in Pluri-Ethnic Cities: An Anthropological Analysis of the Relative Shift from Ethnic tot Supra-Ethnic and Meta-Ethnic Faith Communities in Brussels', Journal of Contemporary Religion, 31 (4): 217-231

Leman, J. (guest ed.) (1999b) 'Education, Ethnic Homogenization and Cultural Hybridization (Brussels, Belgium and Cape Town, South Africa)', International Journal of Educational Research, 31(4): 257-353

Nash, J. (1979) We eat the mines and the mines eat us. New York, Columbia: University Press

Poutignat, P. & Streiff-Fenart, J. (1995) Théories de l'ethnicité. Paris: PUF
Roosens, E. (1989) Creating ethnicity. Newbury Park, London, New Delhi: Sage Publications

Roosens, E., ed. (1995) 'Rethinking culture, "multicultural society" and the school', International Journal of Educational Research, 23(1), 1-105

**CHAPTER III**

Chan, Kwok Bun and Tong, Chee Kiong. (1993) 'Rethinking Assimilation and Ethnicity: The Chinese in Thailand', International Migration Review, 27(1): 140-168

Chang Wen-Chin. (1999) 'Beyond the Military: The Complex Migration and Resettlement of the KMT Yunnanese Chinese in Northern Thailand', Ph. D. dissertation, K.U. Leuven, Belgium

Chang Wen-Chin. (2000) 'The Complexities of Migration and Ethnic Identification of the KMT Yunnanese Chinese in Nothern Thailand', Ethnogia, in press

Daniel, E. V. and Knudsen, J. C. (eds). (1995) Mistrusting Refugees. Berkeley: University of California Press

De Vos, G. A. (1975) 'Ethnic Pluralism: Conflict and Accommodation', in De Vos, G. and Romanucci-Ross, L. (eds.), Ethnic Identity: Cultural Continuities and Change. Palo Alto: Mayfield Publishing Company

Epstein, A. L. (1978) Ethos and Identity. London: Tavistock Publications

Eriksen, T. H. (1993) Ethnicity and Nationalism. London: Pluto Press

Gold, S. J. (1992) Refugee Communities: A Comparative Field Study. Newbury Park, California: Sage Publications

Hansen, A. (1982) 'Self-Settled Rural Refugees in Africa: The Case of Angolans in Zambian Villages', in Hansen, A. and Oliver-Smith, A. (eds.), Involuntary Migration and Resettlement: The Problems and Responses of Dislocated People. Boulder: Westview Press

Hansen, A. and Oliver-Smith, A., (eds.) (1982) Involuntary Migration and Resettlement: The Problems and Responses of Dislocated People. Boulder: Westview Press

Hu, Ch'ing-Jung (Ting, Tsuo-Shao). (1977) Chü pien li hsien chi. Tainan (Taiwan): Tsu yu pao t'ai wan sho

Hutnik, N. (1991) Ethnic Minority Identity: A Social Psychological Perspective. Oxford: Clarendon Press

Kibreab, G. (1987) 'Rural Eritrean Refugees in the Sudan: A Study of the Dynamics of Flight', in Nobel, P. (ed.), Refugees and Development in Africa. Uppsala: Scandinavian Institute of African Studies

Kunz, E. F. (1973) 'The Refugee in Flight: Kinetic Models and Forms of Displacement', International Migration Review, 7(2): 125-164

Kunz, E. F. (1981) 'Exile and Resettlement: Refugee Theory.' International Migration Review, 15(1): 42-51

Knudsen, J. C. (1988) Vietnamese Survivors: Processes Involved in Refugee Coping and Adaptation. Migration Project, Department of Social Anthropology, University of Bergen, Denmark

Mangalam, J. J. (1968) Human Migration: A Guide to Migration Literature in English 1955-1962. Lexington: University of Kentucky Press

Ministry of Defense, Taiwan. (1964) Tien mien pien chü iu chi chan shih. Taipei: Kuo fang pu shih Chêng Chü

Ministry of Information, the Union of Burma. (1953) The Kuomintang Aggression against Burma. Rangoon: Ministry of Information

Prakatwuttisan, K. (1995) Gong phon gaw sib sam bon ban phatang. Chiang Mai: Siam Rat Publishing Co

Roosens, E. (1989) Creating Ethnicity: The Process of Ethnogenesis. Newbury Park: Sage Publications

Scudder, T. and Colson, E. (1982) 'From Welfare to Development: A Conceptual Framework for the Analysis of Dislocated People', in Hansen, A. and Oliver-Smith, A. (eds.), Involuntary Migration and Resettlement: The Problems and Responses of Dislocated People. Boulder: Westview Press

Shami, S. (1993) 'The Social Implications of Population Displacement and Resettlement: An Overview with a Focus on the Arab Middle East', International Migration Review, 22(1): 4-33

T'an, Wei-Chên. (1984) Yün nan fan kung ta hsüeh shiao shih. Kaoshiung: Ch'ên shiang ch'u pan sho

Yawnghwe, Chao Tzang. (1987) The Shan of Burma: Memories of a Shan Exile. Singapore: Institute of Southeast Asian Studies

Young, K. R. (1970) Nationalist Chinese Troops in Burma: Obstacle in Burma's Foreign Relations, 1949-1961. Ph. D. dissertation, New York University

**CHAPTER IV**

Anschutz, H. (1985) Die Syrischen Christen vom Tur'Abdin, Eine Altchristliche Bevölkungsgruppe Zwischen Beharrung, Stagnation und Auflösung. Verlag Würzburg: Augustinus

Arkoun, M. (1989) Ouvertures sur l'islam. Paris: Grancher

Armstrong, J. (1982) Nations before Nationalism. Chapel Hill: The University of North Carolina Press

Barth, F. (ed.) (1969) Ethnic Groups and Boundaries: the Social Organisation of Culture Difference. Oslo, Bergen, Tromso: Universitetsforlaget

Bjorklund, U. (1981) North to another country. The formation of a suryoyo community in Sweden. Stockholm: Studies in Social Anthropology

Chabry, L. & A. (1987) Politique et minorités au Proche-Orient, les raisons d'une explosion. Paris: ed. Maisonneuve & Larose

De Vos, G. & L. Romanucci-Ross (eds.) (1975) Ethnic Identity: Cultural Continuities and Change. CA, Palo Alto: Mayfield Publishing Co

Dolgin, J., D. Kemnitzer & D. Schneider (ed.) (1977) Symbolic Anthropology, A Reader in the Study of Symbols and Meanings. New York: Columbia University Press

Gardet, L. (1961) La cité muselmanne. Vie sociale et politique. Paris: Vrin

Katzir, Y. (1982) Preservation of Jewish Ethnic Identity in Yemen: Segregation and Integration as Boundary Maintenance Mechanisms, in: Comparative Studies in Society and History, an international Quarterly, vol.24,nr.2

Le Goff, J. (1984) La civilisation de l'Occident médiéval. Paris: Les Editions Arthaud, 1984

Platti, E. (1995) Nationalisme en islam, in: Is God een Turk ? Nationalisme en Religie, Burghgraeve e.a., Leuven: Davidsfonds

Smith, A.D. (1981) The ethnic revival. Cambridge University Press

Smith, A.D. (1991) National Identity. London: Pinguin Books Ltd

Sumer, F. (1982) De Syrisch-orthodoxe gemeenschap. Hengelo: Bar Hebreaus

Valognes, J-P. (1994) Vie et mort des chrétiens d'orient, Des origines à nos jours. Paris: Librairie Arthème Fayard

Van Den Berghe, P., 1987 (1981) The Ethnic Phenomenon. New York: Praeger Publishers

Yacoub, J. (1985) Les Assyro-Chaldéens. Un Peuple oublié de l'histoire. Paris: Groupement pour les Droits des Minorités, ed. Fayard

**CHAPTER V**

Armstrong, J.A. (1982) Nations before Nationalism. Chapel Hill: The University of North Carolina Press

Balint, A. (1992) Kelemen tanar ur elöadasa a Magyargyerömonostori templomrol, Mànàstireni

Barany, G. (1981) On Truth in Myths, in East European Quarterly, Vol. XV, no.3, September, 347-355

Basa, E.M. (1993) Hungarian Literature: An Introductory Survey, in Paolucci, A. (ed. ) Hungarian Literature, New York: Griffon House Publications, 20-31

Beck, S. (1989) The Origin of Gypsy Slavery in Romania, in Dialectical Anthropology 14, 53-61

Buckley, A. & Nixon, P., (1998) Fantasy, rumour, social cohesion and inter-group tension in Transylvania. Established and Outsiders in the Gurghiu Valley, in: Kürti L. & Fox J. (eds.) Beyond Borders. New York: Colombia University Press

Crowe, D. (1989) The Gypsy Historical Experience in Romania, in Crowe, D. & Kolsti, J. (eds.) The Gypsies of Eastern Europe, Armonk/New York: M.E. Sharpe, 61-79

Cushing, G.F. (1993) The Role of the National Poet, in Paolucci, A. (ed.) Hungarian Literature, New York: Griffon House Publications, 59-80

Detrez, R. (1992) De Balkan. Van burenruzie tot burgeroorlog. Antwerpen/Baarn: Hadewijch

Draganescu, M. (1994) Le retour de la langue roumaine dans son espace latin, in Bulletin de l'Académie Royale de langue et de littérature françaises, Tome 72, no. 3-4, 343-358

Giurescu, C.C. (1967) Transilvania în istoria poporului român. Bucuresti: Editura stiintificà

Glatz, F. (1983) Backwardness, Nationalism, Historiography, in East European Quarterly, XVII, no.1, March, 31-40

Hancock, I. (1989) The East European Roots of Romani Nationalism, in Crowe, D. & Kolsti, J. (eds.) The Gypsies of Eastern Europe, Armonk/New York: M.E. Sharpe, 133-150

Hitchins, K. (1983) Studies on Romanian National Consciousness. Roma: Nagard Publisher Istoria românilor din cele mai veche timpuri pînà la revolutia din 1821, (1994) Manuel pentru clasa a VII-a, Ministerul învàtàmântului. Bucuresti: Editura didacticà si pedagogicà

Köpeczi, B. (ed.) (1994) History of Transylvania. Budapest: Akadémiai Kiado. Translated from Hungarian by A. Chambers-Makkai, e.a.

Pascu, S. (1982) A History of Transylvania. Detroit: Wayne State University Press. Translated from Hungarian by D. Robert Ladd.

Pilon, J.G. (1992) The Bloody Flag. Post-Communist Nationalism in Eastern Europe. Spotlight on Romania. New Brunswick: Transaction Publishers

Pomogats, B. (1993) Hungarian Literatures Beyond the Borders, in Paolucci, A. (ed.), Hungarian Literature, New York: Griffon House Publications, 99-118

Prodan, D. (1971) Supplex Libellus Valachorum or The Political Struggle of the Romanians in Transylvania during the 18th Century. (Bibliotheca Historica Romaniae Monographs VIII), Bucharest: Publishing House of the Academy of the Socialist Republic of Romania

Radulescu, A. (1990) Imnul de stat al României. Bucuresti: Editura muzicalà

Recensàmîntul populatiei si locuintelor. Rezultate preliminare 7.01.1992, (iunie 1992), Bucuresti: Comisia Nationalà pentru statisticà

Rus, C.T. (1994) Monografia satului Mànàsturu-românesc. Tezà de licentà in Teologie, Cluj-Napoca: Universitatea Babes-Bolyai, Facultatea de Teologie pastoralà. Unedited theses

Schipper, J. (1992) Neem nou Budapest. Utrecht: A.W. Bruna Uitgevers

Schöpflin, G. (1974) Rumanian Nationalism, in Survey. A Journal of Soviet and East European Studies, London, Vol. 20, no. 5, 77-104

Schöpflin, G. & Poulton, H. (April 1990) Romania's Ethnic Hungarians. A report by the Minority Rights Group, London: Expedite Graphic Limited

Shafir, M. (1994) Ethnic Tension Runs High in Romania, in RFE/RL Research Report, Vol. 3, no. 32, 19 August, 24-32

Szönyi, G. E. (1993) The Emergence of Major Trends and Themes in Hungarian Literature, in Paolucci, A. (ed.), Hungarian Literature, New York: Griffon House Publications, 32-58

The Romanian Research Group (1977) On Transylvanian Ethnicity. A Reply to Ethnocide in Romania, in Current Anthropology, 20, no. 1, 135-140

Vasaru, F. (1961) Monografia folklorică a comunei Mànàstireni. Lucrare de diploma, Cluj: Universitatea Babes-Bolyai, Facultatea de Filologie. Unedited theses

Vékony, G. (1989) The Theory of Daco-Rumanian Continuity. The origin of the Rumanians and the settlement of Transylvania, in The New Hungarian Quarterly, no. 110, 118-125

Verdery, K. (1983) Transylvanian Villagers. Three Centuries of Political, Economic and Ethnic Change. Berkeley/Los Angeles: University of California Press

Vogel, S. (1994) Transylvania: Myth and Reality, Changing Awareness of Transylvanian Identity, in Gerrits, A. & Adler, N. (eds.), Vampires Unstaked. National Images, Stereotypes and Myths in East Central Europe. Amsterdam: Koninklijke Nederlandse Akademie van Wetenschappen, 67-87

Wass, A. (1979) Selected Hungarian Legends. Florida: Danubian Press. Translated from Hungarian by Elizabeth Wass de Czege

Wesselink, E. (1992) De grieks-katholieke kerk in Roemenië, in Oost-Europa Verkenningen, no.120, March/April, 41-49

**CHAPTER VI**

Aranzadi, J. (1981) Milenarismo vasco: Edad de oro, etnia y nativismo. Madrid: Taurus

Araya, G. (1983) El pensamiento de Américo Castro: Estructura intercastiza de la historia de España. Madrid: Alianza Editorial

Arié, R. (1987) Historia de España (M. Tuñón de Lara, ed.). Part III: España musulmana (siglos VIII-XV). Barcelona: Labor

Asensio, E. (1976) La España imaginada de Américo Castro. Barcelona: El Albir

Avilés Fernández, M. (1980) 'Motivos de crítica a la Inquisición en tiempos de Carlos V (aportaciones para una historia de la oposición a la Inquisición)', pp. 165-192 in: J. Pérez Villanueva (ed.), La Inquisición española. Nueva visión, nuevos horizontes. Siglo XXI, Madrid

Bataillon, M. (1966) Erasmo y España: Estudios sobre la historia espiritual del siglo XVI. Mexico-Buenos Aires: Fondo de cultura económica

Behar, R. (1986) Santa María del Monte: the presence of the past in a Spanish village. Princeton (New Jersey): Princeton University Press

Bennassar, B. (1984) Inquisición española: poder político y control social. Barcelona: Crítica Editorial

Bobillo, F. (1981) Nacionalismo gallego. La ideología de Vicente Risco. Madrid: Akal

Boxer, C. R. (1978) The Church Militant and Iberian Expansion (1440-1770). Baltimore and London: The John Hopkins University Press

Calvo Buezas, T. (1995) Crece el racismo, también la solidaridad. Madrid: Tecnos

Cardaillac, L. (1977) Morisques et Chrétiens. Un affrontement polémique (1492-1640). Paris: Librairie Klincksieck

Cardaillac, L. (ed.) (1991) Tolède, XIIe-XIIIe: Musulmans, chrétiens et juifs: le savoir et la tolérance. Paris: Editions Autrement

Caro Baroja, J. (1978 a) Las formas complejas de la vida religiosa: Religión, sociedad y carácter en la España de los siglos XVI y XVII. Madrid: Akal

Caro Baroja, J. (1978 b) Los judíos en la España Moderna y Contemporánea. Parts II and III. Madrid: Istmo

Caro Baroja, J. (1985) Los moriscos del reino de Granada. Madrid: Istmo

Caro Baroja, (1986) Los judíos en la España Moderna y Contemporánea. Part I. Madrid: Istmo

Caro Baroja, J. (1990) Razas, pueblos y linajes. Murcia: Universidad de Murcia

Castro, A. (1971) La realidad histórica de España. Mexico: Editorial Porrúa

Castro, A. (1972) De la edad conflictiva: Crisis de la cultura española en el siglo XVII. Madrid: Taurus

Castro, A. (1974) Cervantes y los casticismos españoles. Madrid: Alianza

Castro, A. (1983) España en su historia. Cristianos, moros y judíos. Madrid: Editorial Crítica

Castro, A. (1987) La realidad histórica de España. Mexico: Editorial Porrúa

Cátedra Tomás, M. (1989) La vida y el mundo de los vaqueiros de Alzada. Madrid: Siglo XXI de España Editores

Chauchadis, C. (1984) Honneur, morale et société dans l'Espagne de Philippe II. Paris: Editions du C.N.R.S.

Colomer, J. M. (1986) Cataluña como cuestión de Estado. La idea de nación en el pensamiento político catalán (1939-1979). Madrid: Tecnos

Cuenca Toribio, J. M. (1991) Ensayos sobre Andalucía. Córdoba: Caja Provincial de Ahorros de Córdoba

Domínguez Ortiz, A. (1983) Andalucía ayer y hoy. El presente andaluz visto a través de su evolución histórica. Barcelona: Planeta

Domínguez Ortiz, A. (1985) Instituciones y sociedad en la España de los Austrias. Barcelona: Ariel

Domínguez Ortiz, A. (1986) 'El problema judío', pp. 29-37 in: Historia 16, 10° aniversario

Domínguez Ortiz, A. (1988) Los judeoconversos en España y América. Madrid: Istmo

Domínguez Ortiz, A. (1991) "Andalucía ante el 92", pp.178-184 in: Historia 16, no.181

Domínguez Ortiz, A. and Vincent B. (1978) Historia de los moriscos. Vida y tragedia de una minoría. Madrid : Biblioteca de la Revista de Occidente

Fraser, R. (1979) Blood of Spain: The Experience of Civil War, 1936-1939. Middlesex: Penguin Books

Freeman, S. Tax (1968) 'Religious Aspects of the Social Organization of a Castilian Village', pp. 34-49 in: American Anthropologist, 70 (1)

Frigolé, J. et al. (1983) Antropología, hoy. Una introducción a la antropología cultural. Barcelona: Editorial Teide

García Morente, M. (1943) Ideas para una filosofía de la Historia de España. Madrid: Universidad de Madrid

Glick, T. (1991) Cristianos y musulmanes en la España medieval (711-1250). Madrid: Alianza Universidad

Gómez-Martínez, J. L. (1975) Américo Castro y el origen de los españoles: historia de una polémica. Madrid: Gredos

Horst, H. (1985) Castilla y Cataluña en el debate cultural: 1714-1939. Barcelona: Ediciones Península

Jiménez Lozano, J. (1966) Meditación española sobre la libertad religiosa. Barcelona: Ediciones Destino

Kamen, H. (1980) Spain in the later Seventeenth Century (1665-1700). London-New York: Longman

Kamen, H. (1985) Inquisition and Society in Spain: in the XVI and XVII Centuries. Frome and London: Butler & Tanner

Kamen, H. (1986) 'Una crisis de conciencia en la Edad de Oro en España: Inquisición contra 'limpieza de sangre'', pp. 321-356 in: Bulletin Hispanique, LXXXVII, 3-4

Kenny, M. (1969) A Spanish Tapestry: Town and Country in Castile. Gloucester: Peter Smith

Ladero Quesada, M. A. (1979) Granada. Historia de un país islámico (1232-1571). Madrid: Gredos

Lannon, F. (1987) Priviledge, Persecution, and Prophecy. The Catholic Church in Spain 1875-1975. Oxford: Clarendon Press

Lea, H. C. (1983) Historia de la Inquisición española. 2 volumes. Madrid: Fundación Universitaria Española

Le Flem, J. P. et al. (1984) Historia de España (M. Tuñón de Lara, ed.). Part V: La frustración de un imperio (1476-1714). Barcelona: Labor

Lipschutz, A. (1975) El problema racial en la conquista de América. Mexico: Siglo XXI

Lisón-Tolosana, C. (1983) Belmonte de los Caballeros: Anthropology and History in an Aragonese Community. Princeton: Princeton University Press

López-Pintor, R. and J. I. Wert Ortega (1982) 'La otra España. Insolidaridad e intolerancia en la tradición político-cultural española', pp. 7-25 in: Revista Española de Investigaciones Sociológicas, 19

Máiz, R. (1984, a) O rexionalismo galego: organización e ideoloxía (1886-1907). A Coruña: Ediciós do Castro

Máiz, R. (1984, b) 'Raza y mito céltico en los orígenes del nacionalismo gallego: Manuel M. Murguía', pp. 137-180 in: Revista Española de Investigaciones Sociológicas, 25

Marías, J. (1987) España inteligible. Razón histórica de las Españas. Madrid: Alianza

Márquez Villanueva, F. (1984) 'El problema historiográfico de los moriscos', pp. 61-135 in: Bulletin Hispanique, LXXXVI, 1-2

Márquez Villanueva, F. (1994) El concepto cultural alfonsí. Madrid: Mapfre

Menéndez Pelayo, M. (1911) Historia de los heterodoxos españoles. Part I. Madrid: Librería general de Victoriano Suárez

Menéndez Pelayo, M. (1917) Historia de los heterodoxos españoles. Parts II and III. Madrid: Librería general de Victoriano Suárez

Menéndez Pelayo, M. (1947) Historia de los heterodoxos españoles. Parts III, IV and VII. Madrid: C.S.I.C.

Menéndez Pelayo, M. (1948) Historia de los heterodoxos españoles. Parts V, VI and VIII. Madrid: C.S.I.C.

Menéndez Pidal, R. (ed.) (1989) Historia de España. Part XIX. Madrid: Espasa-Calpe

Menéndez Pidal, R. (ed.) (1990) Historia de España. Part XIII (2 vol.). Madrid: Espasa-Calpe

Monroe, J. T. (1970) Islam and the Arabs in Spanish Scholarship (Sixteenth Century to the Present). Leiden: E. J. Brill

Monsalvo Antón, J. M. (1985) Teoría y evolución de un conflicto social. El antisemitismo en la Corona de Castilla en la Baja Edad Media. Madrid: Siglo XXI

Moxó y Ortiz de Villajos, S. de and M. A. Ladero Quesada (ed.) (1984) Historia de España y América. Part IV: La España de los cinco Reinos (1085-1369). Madrid: Ediciones Rialp

Ortega y Gasset, J. (1984) España invertebrada. Madrid: Espasa-Calpe

Payne, S. G. (1984) El catolicismo español. Barcelona: Planeta

Racionero, L. (1987) España en Europa: El fin de la 'edad conflictiva' y el cambio de rumbo de la sociedad española. Barcelona: Planeta

Revah, I. (1971) 'Les controverses sur les statuts de pureté de sang', pp. 263-306 in: Bulletin Hispanique, LXXIII

Selke, A. (1980) 'El iluminismo de los conversos y la Inquisición. Cristianismo interior de los alumbrados: resentimiento y sublimación', pp. 617-636 in: Pérez Villanueva, J., La Inquisición española. Nueva visión, nuevos horizontes. Madrid: Siglo XXI

Sicroff, A. (1960) Les controverses des statuts de 'pureté de sang' en Espagne du XVe au XVII siècle. Paris: Didier

Smith, A. D. (1986) The ethnic Origins of Nations. Oxford: Basil Blackwell

Smith, A. D. (1992) 'Chosen peoples: why ethnic groups survive', pp. 436-456 in: Ethnic and Racial Studies, 15 (3)

Solé, C. (1980) 'Identificación de los inmigrantes con la cultura catalana', pp. 119-138 in: Revista Española de Investigaciones Sociológicas, 9

Solé, C. (1981) 'Integración versus catalanización de los inmigrantes', pp. 171-197 in: Sistema, 43-44

Stallaert, C. (1996) Etnisch nationalisme in Spanje. De historisch-antropologische grens tussen christenen en Moren. Leuven: Leuven University Press

Stallaert, C. (1998) Etnogénesis y etnicidad en España. Barcelona: Proyecto A

Suárez Fernández, L. (ed.) (1981) Historia General de España y América. Part V: Los Trastámara y la unidad española (1369-1517). Madrid: Ediciones Rialp

Todorov, T. (1982) La conquête de l'Amérique. La question de l'autre. Paris: Editions du Seuil

Trías Vejarano, J. J. (1975) Almirall y los orígenes del catalanismo. Madrid: Siglo XXI

Tuñón de Lara, M., J. Valdeón Baruque and A. Domínguez Ortiz (1991) Historia de España. Barcelona: Labor

Vilar, P. (1982) Hidalgos, amotinados y guerrilleros: Pueblo y poderes en la historia de España. Barcelona: Editorial Crítica

**CHAPTER VII**

Ardener, E. (1989) 'The Construction of History: "vestiges of creation"', in Tonkin, E. (ed.), History and Ethnicity, ASA Monographs, London and New York: Routledge, 22-33

Armstrong, J.A. (1982) Nations before Nationalism. Chapel Hill: The University of North Caroline Press

Bafekr, S. & Leman, J. (1999) 'Highly-qualified Iranian immigrants in Germany: the role of ethnicity and culture', Journal of Ethnic and Migration Studies, 25(1): 95-112

Barth, F. (1969) Ethnic Groups and Boundaries: the Social Organisation of Culture Difference. Oslo, Bergen, Tromso: Universitetsforlaget

Brass, P. (1991) Ethnicity and Nationalism. Theory and Comparison. New Delhi, Newbury Park, London: Sage Publications

174

Chapman, M., McDonald, M. and E. Tonkin (1989) 'Introduction', in Tonkin, E. (ed.), History and Ethnicity, ASA Monographs, London and New York: Routledge, 1-21

De Certeau, M. (1988) The Writing of History. New York: Columbia University Press; translated from French: L'écriture de l'histoire. Paris: Gallimard (1975)

De Vos, G. (1975) 'Ethnic Pluralism: Conflict and Accomodation', in De Vos, G. and L. Romanucci-Ross, eds., Ethnic Identity. Cultural Continuities and Change. Mayfield, Palo Alto, CA

Drummond, L. (1980) 'The cultural continuum: a theory of intersystems', Man, vol. 15(2)

Epstein, A.L. (1978) Ethos and Identity. London: Tavistock Publications; Chicago: Aldine Publications

Eriksen, T.H. (1993) Ethnicity & Nationalism. London: Pluto Press

Fischer, M.M.J. (1986) in Marcus, G.E. and Fischer, M.M.J., Anthropology as Cultural Critique. An experimental moment in the human sciences. Chicago: University of Chicago Press, 176

Friedman, J. (1992) 'The Past in the Future: History and the Politics of Identity', American Anthropologist, vol. 94(4), 837-859

Gans, H. (1994) 'Symbolic ethnicity and symbolic religiosity: towards a comparison of ethnic and religious acculturation', Ethnic and Racial Studies, vol. 17(4), 577-592

Grosby, S. (1994) 'The verdict of history: the inexpungeable tie of primordiality - a response to Eller and Coughlan', Ethnic and Racial Studies, vol. 17(1), 164-171

Horowitz, D.L. (1975) 'Ethnic Identity', in Glazer, N. and D.P. Moynihan, eds., Ethnicity: Theory and Experience. Harvard University Press, Cambridge, MA, 111-140

Horowitz, D.L. (1985) Ethnic Groups in conflict. Berkeley, Los Angeles & London: University of California Press

Leach, E. (1954) Political systems of Highland Birma. London: G.Bell

Le Goff, J. (1977) Pour un autre Moyen Age. Temps, travail et culture en Occident. Paris: Gallimard

Leman, J. (1990) 'Multilingualism as norm, monolingualism as exception: the Foyer Model in Brussels' in Byram, M. and Leman, J. (eds.) Bicultural and Trilingual Education. Clevedon - Philadelphia: Multilingual Matters

Leman, J. (1991) Intégrité, intégration. Brussels, De Boeck University

Leman, J. (1997) 'Undocumented migrants in Brussels: diversity and anthropological rationale', New Community, Vol. 23, n.1, 25-41

Leman, J. (1998) 'The Italo-Brussels Jehovah's Witnesses Revisited: from first-generation religious fundamentalism to ethno-religious community formation', Social Compass, 45(2): 219-226

LeVine, R.A. and Campbell, D.T. (1972) Ethnocentrism: Theories of Conflict, Ethnic Attitudes, and Group Behaviour. New York: J. Wiley & Sons

McKay, J. (1982) 'An exploratory synthesis of primordial and mobilizationist approaches to ethnic phenomena', Ethnic and Racial Studies, vol. 5(4), 395-420

Patterson, O. (1975) 'Contact and Choice in Ethnic Allegiance: A Theoretical Framework and Carribbean Case Study', in Glazer, N. and D.P. Moynihan, eds. Ethnicity: Theory and Experience. Harvard University Press, Cambridge, MA, 305-349

Paulston, C.B. (1987) 'Conséquences linguistiques de l'ethnicité et du nationalisme dans des contextes plurilingues', X.X. (CERI), L'éducation multiculturelle. Paris: OCDE

Poutignat, P. & Streiff-Fenart, J. (1995) Théories de l'ethnicité. Paris: P.U.F.

Roosens, E.E. (1989) Creating Ethnicity: The Process of Ethnogenesis. Newbury Park, London, New Delhi: Sage Publications

Sahlins, M. (1985) Islands of History. Chicago & London: The University of Chicago Press

Scott, G. (1990) 'A resynthesis of the primordial and circumstancialist approaches to ethnic group solidarity: towards an explanatory model', Ethnic and Racial Studies, vol. 13(2), 147-171

Silverman, S. (1979) 'On the Uses of History in Anthropology: "The Palio" of Siena', American Anthropologist, vol.6 (3), 413-435

Smith, A.D. (1981) The Ethnic Revival. Cambridge University Press

Smith, A.D. (1986) The Ethnic Origins of Nations. Oxford: Basil Blackwell

Smith, A.D. (1991) National Identity. London: Pinguinb Books Ltd

Smith, A.D. (1992) 'Chosen peoples: why ethnic groups survive', Ethnic and Racial Studies, vol. 15(3), 436-456

Spicer, E. (1971) 'Persistent Cultural Systems, A comparative study of identity systems that can adapt to contrasting environments' Science, vol. 4011, 795-800

Wilson, R. (1993) 'Anchored communities: Identity and History of the Maya - Q'eqchi' Man, vol. 28(1)

Yang, C.K. (1991) Religion in Chinese Society. Taipei: SMC Publishing Inc.

# BIOGRAPHICAL NOTES

Chang Wen Chin (°1964), Ph.D. in Social and Cultural Anthropology at the Catholic University of Leuven, with a thesis on "Beyond the Military: the Complex Migration and Resettlement of the KMT Yunnanese Chinese in Northern Thailand" (1999). Member of MERIB.

Ghequière Kathleen (°1958), Ph.D. in Social and Cultural Anthropology at the Catholic University of Leuven, with a thesis on religion, ethnicity and interethnic relations among the christian Suryoye refugee immigrants from Southeast Turkey and among catholic Vietnamese refugee immigrants in Brussels.

Leman Johan (°1946), Ph.D. in Social and Cultural Anthropology, is professor at the Department of Social and Cultural Anthropology and at the Center for European Studies of the Catholic University of Leuven; director of the federal Center of Equal Opportunities and Opposition to Racism in Brussels; president of Foyer, regional center for minorities in Brussels. Belgian member at the European monitoring centre for racism and xenophobia (Vienna) and Belgian member at the European Commission against racism and intolerance (Strasbourg). Publications on Mediterranean cultures, bicultural education, interethnic relations, undocumented migrants. Director of MERIB.

Stallaert Christiane (°1959), Ph.D. in Social and Cultural Anthropology at the Catholic University of Leuven, is professor of Spanish at the Higher Institute for Translators and Interpreters at the University of Antwerp. Publications on migration, interethnic relations and nationalism. Author of "Etnogénesis y etnicidad en España" (Barcelona, 1998), in Dutch: "Etnisch nationalisme in Spanje" (Leuven University Press, 1996). Member of MERIB.

Van de Vyver Greet (°1967), Ph.D. in Social and Cultural Anthropology at the Catholic University of Leuven, with a thesis on "Transilvaanse dorpsculturen in een smeltbron van historische entiteiten" (Transilvanian village cultures in a melting pot of historical traditions). (1999). Member of MERIB.

Peter Lang · Europäischer Verlag der Wissenschaften

Andrzej Radziewicz-Winnicki

# Tradition and Reality in Educational Ethnography of Post-Communist Poland

**Essays in Sociology of Education and Social Pedagogy**

Frankfurt/M., Berlin, Bern, New York, Paris, Wien, 1998. 168 pp.
ISBN 3-631-32691-2 · pb. DM 59.–*
US-ISBN 0-8204-3547-3

The educational and cultural determinants of the tempo and direction of transformation of the democratic and the normative order in post-totalitarian society are analysed. The Author's analyses presented in this book attempt to answer the following question: How does one pass from normative order to normative integration? Which properties of the new systemic educational identity are conductive to the active creation of social normative order in Poland? What is the religious adaptation to the new state formation? Is it possible in a short time to build in Poland a new pragmatic and progressive educational system based on the unified school which is democratic with unified education and the freedom of choice?

*Contents*: Power and ideology in education · Education and democratic transformation · Destruction and construction of the national culture – institutional effects on religion in Poland · Crisis in educational strategies

Frankfurt/M · Berlin · Bern · New York · Paris · Wien
Distribution: Verlag Peter Lang AG
Jupiterstr. 15, CH-3000 Bern 15
Fax (004131) 9402131
*incl. value added tax
Prices are subject to change without notice.